It's All About You!

It's All About You!

Keri Lynn Siegel

Library of Congress Control Number: 2022902221

HARDBACK: 978-1-957575-35-3
PAPERBACK: 978-1-957575-34-6
EBOOK: 978-1-957575-36-0

Ordering Information:

For orders and inquiries, please contact:
1-888-404-1388
www.goldtouchpress.com
book.orders@goldtouchpress.com

Printed in the United States of America

CONTENTS

Special thanks go to Sally Samuels and all others who have contributed to the successful completion of this book. May God increase your wealth beyond measure and bless you richly in other ways because you believed in me. I love you.

Keri Lynn Siegel

Dedicated to: Dr. Cynthia L. Thompson

Thank you for being a mom to me when my mom and I were not speaking; and thank you for always telling me what you knew I needed to hear. I love you. May God bless you richly.

FROM A PROPHET'S MOUTH TO A SCRIBE'S HEART

It was December 2009. I was homeless, I'd been rejected by those who should have been there to help me, and I was deceived by a man I loved and trusted. My health had come unraveled following my dad's death; and I was taken off the streets by a friend who asked to remain anonymous. Needless to say, I was extremely angry. People who loved me and wanted to help me were having a difficult time being around me because I was lashing out, even at people who didn't deserve it and had nothing to do with my anger. My pastor's wife at Jesus People Proclaim International Ministries Church in Deerfield Beach, FL listened to me for months. Finally, after one evening service, she had to set the boundaries.

Prophet Cynthia L. Thompson has a very unique way of reaching people and of getting people who are not listening to anyone else to listen. God has gifted this classy lady with a way of going right past all your defenses and reaching your heart in a way that you are not expecting. With profound wisdom, she makes you take a step back and think about where you are and what you're doing.

On this December evening in 2009, as I was venting to her; she stood there and patiently waited for me to finish my tangent. Then, she very calmly looked me in the eyes and said, "IT REALLY IS ALL ABOUT YOU... ISN'T IT?" It was one of those moments— one of those life-changing, defining moments. I took a step back and saw myself. I realized in that moment, how self-centered I was being; and how I was blaming everybody else for all the problems in my life, refusing to accept responsibility for any of the issues I had to deal with. I also came to understand that I had real issues that I had to face and it no longer mattered how they came into my life.

Dwelling on the past was not going to set me free or lead me into my freedom in Christ. As long as I continued to live outside of the freedom that He purchased for me, I was selling myself short and grieving the Holy Spirit. I refuse to do that anymore! I knew that if I was going to become who God created me to be, my life had to be all about Him. So, this book was born as I strive to lead myself and others on a journey out of self-centeredness and passing the blame to Christ-centeredness and into Kingdom-centeredness.

SECTION I

"We Have Met the Enemy and he is us"

CHAPTER 1

Pride

Someone once said, "We have met the enemy, and it is us." That is so true. No one can deceive us better than we can deceive ourselves. Pride tells us that everything is alright, that we have nothing to worry about. It tells us that we are right and everyone else is wrong. It keeps us from seeing ourselves as we really are, and it keeps us from seeing ourselves how God sees us. Sometimes, this comes with an air of superiority, often referred to as arrogance. Arrogance makes you act like you are better than a particular individual, group of individuals, or class of people.

Because I came from an upper-middle class family, I believed that all homeless people were either chemically addicted, or were mentally or physically incapable of getting along in normal society. Then, I went through a family crisis and became homeless. After being homeless for nearly two years without finding employment my health unraveled to the point where I was no longer medically cleared to work. It was years after losing this medical clearance to work and after being forced to take a medical leave from the school I had been attending before I was healthy enough for my physicians to approve my resuming my job search and education. During those difficult years, I lost everything all the way down to my pets; but I learned many life-changing lessons, as God had humbled me. James 4:6 says that God resists the proud but gives grace to the humble. Because of that experience, I can talk to anyone who treats me with respect, regardless of whom they are or where they came from. If God is no respecter of persons, who are we to discriminate?

Many who are comfortable in their sin try to use this to make Christians feel that they should never confront sin. That is not the case! Jesus confronted sin wherever He saw it. He unashamedly turned over the moneychangers' tables in the temple (see Mark 11: 15- 19); and He was always challenging the religious leaders of His day because of their hypocrisy. Some of my favorite examples are in Luke 5: 17- 39. When people dealt with their sins openly and honestly, and made a commitment to change their lives; Jesus loved them into a place of restoration, He refused to condemn them, and we are not to either; when they refused to admit they had a problem, their sin remained (see John 8:1-11; and John 9:39-41). If we are to be like Jesus, we must confront sin where we see in it the right way.

The first thing to remember is we are judging the sin, not the person. Matthew 7:1-5 tells us that we will be judged by whatever measure we judge by. Therefore, we need to make sure that our vision and our perspective are clear before we try to help others clear theirs. Then, we need to seek God for the right approach. James 1:5 says, "If any man lacks wisdom, let him ask of God, who gives liberally to all men without finding fault, and it shall be given unto him" (K.J.V.). No one knows how best to reach the other person's heart than Him for He created us all. He knows how we need to confront the other person and the issue, and He knows how the other person needs to hear it. If we are sensitive to the Holy Spirit, the Holy Spirit will give us the right words at the right time. No matter the words we choose, we must speak our words in a heart of love and a spirit of humility– having the same mind as Christ– considering ourselves so we don't fall into the same temptation (see Philippians 2: 5-11; and Galatians 6:1- 2). This does not guarantee that they will respond correctly. All we can do is be obedient to God to do what He has called us to do; and leave the rest to Him. If we see someone in sin, God calls us to warn them, we fail to give them warning, and they die in their sins; God holds us responsible. If we see someone in sin, God calls us to warn them, we give them warning, and they die in their sins; they are responsible for their own failure to repent (see Ezekiel 3: 18- 21). I am most likely to make a mess of my own life when I judge someone else for the mess they have made of theirs. A former mentor of mine used to say, "We can be fruit inspectors", no less and no more.

A sister to pride is false-humility. This deceiving spirit causes you to believe that you deserve to receive the short end of every double standard in your life because everyone is better than you are and you are not qualified to succeed. People who have been through abuse of any kind (physical, mental, emotional, verbal, or sexual) often battle this. I was full of it! I had no idea of whom God had created me to be; and I did not want to know because after a lifetime of insults and verbal abuse, I did not believe I was worth knowing. I thought, "All those people can't be wrong!" They were and they are. Jesus People Proclaim International Ministries Church in Deerfield Beach, FL showed me who God had created me to be and I am thankful. God made me special; and He made you special too. You are worth more than gold because God does not make junk; and that is not just an expression, it is true. He took time to form and fashion you in your mother's womb. You are fearfully and wonderfully made; and so am I (see Isaiah 43: 7; Psalm 119: 73; Psalm 139: 16; and Genesis chapters 1- 2). He thought enough of you to send Jesus to die for you and to put His Spirit inside of you if you have given your life to Christ. If God promised it to you, it belongs to you; and if God says it about you, it is true because there is no opinion that is higher than His (see Isaiah 55:6- 13). No one has the right to keep us down when God is ready to exalt us; and no one has the right to exalt us before God is ready. It is all in His time (see Ecclesiastes 3: 11; and Romans 8: 28).

Even trickier than pride and false-humility is a "false-balance". Proverbs 11:1 says, "A false-balance *is* an abomination to the Lord: but a just weight *is* His delight" (K.J.V.). According to *The Strongest Strong's Exhaustive Concordance of the Bible Hebrew-Aramaic Dictionary*, the Hebrew word used for the word pair "false-balance" is "mirma". It means "deceit, deception, dishonesty, treachery, false, guile, craft, feigned, and subtlety" (James Strong; Zondervan; Grand Rapids, MI; 2001). A false-balance is not only an illusion to others, but it is a way of deceiving ourselves.

This false-balance resembles a pendulum swinging back and forth at full speed, going from one extreme to the other continuously but never coming to rest in the middle. While this dominates the areas of pride and false-humility, it manifests in other areas also. God wants His people to get to a place of peace and rest in Him. Hebrews 4: 9- 11 tells us that there is a rest for the people of God and we need to labor to enter into that rest. "Laboring to enter into rest" seems like a contradiction in terms; but it really is not because all it requires is obedience to whatever God has called us to do. That may vary based upon the circumstances of our lives. When we do what God has called us to do by faith, our labor of faith produces rest. My pastor, Apostle Billy S. Thompson of Jesus People Proclaim International Ministries Church in Deerfield Beach, FL; refers to it as "sweat-less victory".

Those who struggle to find balance outside of Christ end up with false balances in various areas of their lives because The Holy Spirit uses the chaos and confusion they experience in their lives to convict them. Once they turn it over to Him and allow Him to help them bring balance into their lives, they enter into His rest and have peace. Then, their pendulum finally comes to rest in the middle and they experience that sweat-less victory. It takes faith and trust to turn it over, and deal honestly with these false-balances in our lives.

Refusing to deal with these issues in our lives leads to other more self- restricting and self-defeating sins. Furthermore, each sin leads you into deeper self-deception, making it more difficult to become who God has called you to be. The Holy Spirit loves us and He is not willing that any should perish; but that all should come to repentance (see 2 Peter 3:9). Nevertheless, He also is a gentleman and loves us enough to respect our will, even if it breaks His heart. Therefore, if we choose to harden our heart against Him, He will eventually turn away.

An Old Testament example of this is God's dealing with the Pharaoh of Egypt in the book of Exodus. In Chapters 5- chapter 9, verse 7, we see Pharaoh hardening his heart; in Exodus 9:12, the Lord hardened his heart. In the New Testament, we see this reflected in Ananias and Sapphira in Acts 5, and in a more general example in Romans 1. Rebellion and, its similar sin of, lawlessness lead to a multiplicity of other destructive sins. Woe to us, who think we know better than Him and rebel against Him!

Rebellion and lawlessness appear similar; but have subtle differences. What they have in common is that they each lead to more serious sins. Each brings separation from God and distracts you from your true calling and purpose in the earth. Each affects your ability to make a difference in the lives of those you care about. In the end, each will destroy your own happiness, joy, and peace of mind because true happiness and peace of mind only comes from following God and obeying Him in every area of our lives.

Rebellion and lawlessness lead to more false-balances; and more false-balances lead to more rebellion and lawlessness. It becomes a vicious cycle that only the Holy Spirit can deliver us from; but we must be honest and open about where we are and we must be ready and willing to be set free.

If we see signs of rebellion and lawlessness in one or more areas in our heart, if someone brings it to our attention, or if the Holy Spirit brings it forward and we are honest enough to confess our sins to Him, freedom is right around the corner. We have nothing to fear. He is faithful and just to forgive our sins and to cleanse us from all unrighteousness, as promised in 1 John 1:9. He is not a man that He should lie, nor the son of man that He should change his mind, as Numbers 23:19 tells us.

Only those who try to hide their sin from Him are in danger of judgment. He will deliver those who seek Him for the freedom. He is a kind and gracious Savior. That is why Jesus died! He came to set us free! Jesus said, "And you shall know the Truth, and the Truth shall make you free" (see John 8:32). He also proclaimed that He is the Way, the Truth, and the Life; and no one comes to the Father except through Him (see John 14:6). We can only be free in and through Him, by the power of His Spirit; on our own we shall fail. Our pride causes us to believe that we can free ourselves. Jesus told us in John 15, "I Am the true Vine and My Father is the Husbandman. Every branch in Me that beareth not fruit He taketh away: and every *branch* that beareth fruit: He purgeth it, that it may bring forth more fruit. Now, ye are clean through the word, which I have spoken unto you. Abide in Me, and I in you, As the branch cannot bear fruit of itself, except it abide in the vine: no more can ye, except ye abide in me. I Am the Vine, ye *are* the branches: He that abideth in Me, and I in him, the same bringeth forth much fruit: for without Me ye can do nothing" (see verses 1-5).

Our false humility causes us to think that we need to have freed ourselves before we can come to Him. Isaiah describes our righteousness as "filthy rags" (see chapter 64, verse 6). We are powerless without Him; and the sooner we come to terms with that, the sooner we can get free and live the abundant, prosperous life that God has called us to live in Him. Revelation 3 shows us Jesus standing at the door of our lives knocking, wanting to come in. Let Him in so He can do what He does best– bring you the joy that He has called you to.

CHAPTER 2

Lawlessness and Rebellion

Often times, we find in Scripture similar terms that have subtle differences, which unbelievers and new believers do not always notice. Sometimes, maturing believers do not notice these differences for years. It took me nearly 15 years before I learned there was a difference between the soul and spirit. When I read verses like Hebrews 4:12 years ago, I used to inquire about the difference. Finally, someone who did not know any more than I did told me, "I guess it just proves that God is so intimately familiar with us that He can even discern the difference between those," just to shut me up. I was too intellectual at the time for that answer to satisfy me; but I realized that the individual did not know any more than I did and I did not know whom to ask, so I dropped it. Later, I learned that our soul consists of our will, intellect, and emotions; while our spirit is the part of us that responds naturally to the Holy Spirit of God. That is why Jesus said true worshippers will worship Him in spirit and in truth (see John 4:24).

Another example of similar words with distinctive differences in Scripture is "lawlessness" and "rebellion". Scripture speaks of both; and for years, I thought they were the same, but the Holy Spirit opened my eyes to see something. Both have the same result: people who do what they want with no respect for the law. The difference lies in their attitudes behind their actions. Why do they act out?

Some make excuses or try to justify their behavior. They try to get others to side with them. One example might be someone who chooses to go into an area labeled "Staff Only" without proper authorization, simply because they have friends who work in that office. They may try to justify it by saying that they came to see their friend, regardless of whether or not their friend is expecting them. This does not apply to the gray areas where legitimate emergencies occur. For example, the buses I use for my transportation prohibit eating and drinking on the buses. Therefore, I eat before and/or after I get on the buses. However, if while I'm on a bus during a long day where I packed a lunch and I need to eat I do not feel guilty about eating. Other people do not care enough about another's thoughts, feelings, opinions, and ideas to make efforts to explain their actions; but if you try to tell them they are wrong, they may react aggressively either verbally or physically, or file a lawsuit against you. It is a difference in attitude. Many organizations that attack Christian values came out of this spirit of lawlessness. Those making excuses and trying to justify their behavior or getting others to side with them come from a place of rebellion. Those with an "in your face" bold-faced, arrogant attitude are coming from a place of lawlessness.

Lawlessness usually starts out as rebellion. People who have reached a place of lawlessness are not just stubborn; they are bitter. Many have unresolved issues they do not know how to address. One cause maybe jealousy, as in the advisors to King Darius (prince of Persia) who had Daniel thrown into the lion's den because they didn't like that the king favored Daniel {see Daniel chapter 6}. Some have stopped trying to deal with their issues, they simply react. Many religious leaders of Jesus' day had reached a place of lawlessness.

Sometimes, this lawlessness is not obvious until you stumble upon it. I went through a lot in my family, and for years refused to forgive them. While I was doing well in many other areas of my life, whenever others discussed the issue of forgiveness, a lawless spirit raised its head. I had to choose to forgive in order to move forward. Otherwise, I would have remained stuck in the past. My heart grieves for those who cannot get past the past because it's tormenting!

Others stuck in lawlessness are deep into religions and lifestyles going against the design of God. They will file antidiscrimination lawsuits to silence Christians from standing up for what we believe; but today, every population appears to have more freedom of speech than Christians. That was not the intent of the Founding Fathers of this nation. They were Christians who fought to be heard. Fortunately, some within those lifestyles have not become lawless. Some have continued in roots of rebellion, where Romans 1 declares this begins. There is freedom in Christ to those who choose to be free.

Roots of rebellion and lawlessness can manifest in many areas; and even branch out into other roots. Some of these include: greed, idolatry, lust various types of perversions, and many kinds of addictions. Each of these weeds and tares that grow up in a person's life began with a single seed of self-centeredness sown by the devil. Even those who love God and are committed to walking in Him can fall into these areas because the devil is a great deceiver (see Matthew 13:24-30). What makes long-term rebellion and lawlessness so dangerous is how deceptive the devil can be in bringing them into one's life, how difficult they are to see, and how quickly they can interfere with one's salvation. The Holy Spirit proclaims He will not always strive with man (see Genesis 6:3); that is why He brings judgment upon our sins. He is holy and righteous. If He did not judge sin, He could not say that He is holy. We must be sensitive to what He is dealing with in our lives and when He is dealing with them to keep our relationship with Him strong. If we fail to act appropriately, with repentance, to His conviction; it is possible to lose our salvation. Revelation 3 warns two churches (the church of Sardis and the church of Laodicea) that failure to repent may cause their names to be blotted out of "The Book of Life". How do our names get written into "The Book of Life"? That only comes from a relationship with God through Jesus Christ. If our names can be blotted out of the Book of Life, they had to first be there meaning someone must have first had a relationship with Jesus Christ. The fact that their name was "blotted out" or erased means they had to have lost their relationship with Christ. They walked away from Him. Jesus promises that He will never leave us nor forsake us; but if we choose to, we can leave Him and it will break His heart, but He will let us go.

We can lose our salvation through long-term open rebellion because the Spirit of God will not always strive against man. At some point, He will leave us to our own devices. We can also lose our salvation through long-term un- forgiveness or bitterness. Jesus said, in Matthew 6:13-14 that if we refuse to forgive; we cannot be forgiven. Matthew 25:1-13 tells us of certain virgins who were keeping themselves for Him; but when they came before Him, He told them, "I know you not" while in Matthew 7:20-23 Jesus tells some who thought they were in right standing with Him (because they were doing good deeds in His Name) "I never knew you". There is a clear difference! Matthew 25:31-46 shows us that those who are facing eternal judgment because they have failed to maintain their walk with Him will receive the same punishment as the devil and his demons. Finally, in Mark 3:29, we are warned that the blasphemy against the Holy Spirit will not be forgiven. According to *The Strongest Strong's Exhaustive Concordance of the Bible Greek Dictionary Index to the New Testament*, by James Strong, the Greek word for "blasphemy" is "blasphemeo"; and it means "to insult, slander, curse, speak evil of, defame, and revile" (Zondervan Publications; Grand Rapids, MI; 2001). The Lord makes it clear in Matthew 10:22 that it is only those who endure until the end who will be saved. Matthew 24:13 and Hebrews 10:26-39 supports this. God is looking for consistency in His people. He will not let go of us; but we can let go of Him. Hang onto Him as if your life and soul depend upon Him because it does!

If you have chosen to walk away from Him and you are reading this, there is still hope for you. All you have to do is confess your sin to Him– whether it is un-forgiveness or some other form of long-term rebellion, surrender your will and all your controls to Him, and listen to obey Him. If we are open and honest about our sins, He is faithful and just to forgive our sins and to cleanse us from all unrighteousness. He will make us new and give us a new start. "If any man is in Christ, he is a new creation. Old things have passed away. Behold, all things have become new" (see 2 Corinthians 5:17). That gives you the right and everyone around you who calls themselves a follower of Christ, the requirement to let it go. Even the devil can no longer hold it against you. If the devil tries to bring it back to you, tell him, "Shut up, devil! It's under The Blood! I no longer have to be bound by that! I'm not listening to you anymore!" However, if you choose to deny your sins, your sins will be retained– like the religious leaders of Jesus' day trying to claim that they were free of sin (see John 9:39-41; and 1 John 1:5-10). Luke 15:4-7 reveals that there is more rejoicing in Heaven over one sinner who repents than over 99 righteous people who do not think they need to. Jesus declared that it is the sick that need a doctor (see Matthew 9:12), revealing that He came for the lost (see Matthew 18:11). Do not forget that; and do not forget where we came from.

CHAPTER 3

Secondary Motivators for Idolatry

The Bible gives many warnings against idolatry. There is only One God; and we cannot make Him in our image. Many people attempt to anyway. Rebellion and lawlessness are primary motivators for their idolatry. What are the secondary motivators for pursuing this lifestyle? How does it manifest in people's lives? It is important to understand that there are two main classifications of idols: "idols of love" and "idols of fear". The "idols of love" are idols you compromise for because your love for them becomes greater than your love for God. You treasure these and worry if you do not submit to their demands or desires, you might lose them. So, instead of trusting God, you compromise your values. You are so terrified of your "idols of fear" that you compromise your values to keep them happy in order to avoid their wrath. You are actually walking on proverbial "eggshells" around them, because they intimidate you so much that you have difficulty trusting God with them. In each of these cases, you might not actually be standing or kneeling before a statue; but you may as well be because, in the spiritual realm, you are. We must come to a place of courage and strength in the Lord and stand against these idols. Ephesians 6:10-18 commands us to be strong in the Lord and in the power of His might, to put on the whole armor of God so we may stand against all the fiery darts of the wicked one, and then it details for us what the holy arsenal is that God has given to His children. He has not left us defenseless. He knew we would need help and made sure we had it. We also have all of Heaven backing us up.

If love and fear were the only secondary motivators for idolatry, it would be great. Unfortunately, there are others; and our hearts can deceive us (see Jeremiah 17:9-10). We often are unaware of what we are thinking until the Holy Spirit convicts us; but if we are honest and open before Him, we can be free. One issue that comes up a lot is greed. People, who think of greed, usually relate it to money; but greed can be transferred to anything. For example: some covet another's spouse and end up having an affair. Some covet another's business and end up bankrupting their business partners. These are only examples. The list is endless. In the end, Proverbs 15:27 tells us, "He that is greedy of gain troubleth his own house: but he that hateth gifts shall live" (K.J.V.). The giving and receiving of bribes are one manifestation of greed in a person's heart.

Another secondary motivator for idolatry is lust. It begins with coveting someone else's spouse; but if it stopped there, it wouldn't turn into an affair. Unfortunately, sin that is not dealt with is left to progress into far worse sins. That's why, Proverbs 19:18 exhorts us to discipline our children while there is time. Otherwise, we will wish we did. The priest Eli in 1 Samuel chapter 3 is an example of this. Lust is simply greed that became an obsession. Unfortunately, people usually limit greed to financial matters and lust to sexual matters in their thinking; but both can cross each spectrum. That is what makes each morally and spiritually dangerous. 1 Corinthians 10:6 tells us we should not lust after evil, which is pretty inclusive.

Even at the stage of lust, no one has acted upon the evil they have not been obsessively thinking about. Of course, Jesus says in Matthew 5, that if you have thought about it, you have already done it in your heart; so you have in God's eyes. If man had God's standards, there would be less crime! The first sign that the greed and lust are acted upon is perversion, which people also think of as being strictly sexual. Unfortunately, justice can be perverted also— when the laws are skewed to benefit a certain class of people who are more advantaged or have more political clout. This does not always happen; but when it does, justice was perverted. That is the nature of political scandals. Some become publicized; others do not.

In the King James Version, it's typically translated "froward" when perversion manifests in non-sexual ways. The King James translation of "frowardness" or "froward" is defined as "to be devious, be perverse, be deceitful; or to depart (from one's sight)" (Strong, James; *The Strongest Strong's Exhaustive Concordance of the Bible Hebrew- Aramaic Dictionary-Index to the Old Testament*; Zondervan Publications; Grand Rapids, MI; 2001). People who have become froward have become crooked in their dealings. As their thinking becomes more froward, their actions become more perverted because their thinking is twisted by the wicked one who has them deceived. They think all is well; and everything is normal. Little do they know they have fallen into the dark traps of the evil one; and without someone to shine the light of Christ for them, they may be lost for eternity. This lost soul does not understand that he or she is lost. He or she may become defensive about it. No one wants to believe he is in denial to a problem he cannot see. Furthermore, a paraphrase of a verse from Proverbs says, "He who sets a trap for others will eventually end up in his own trap," so the consequences of his or her froward lifestyle are extremely destructive not only to others, but also to himself or herself.

All of this perversion and froward thinking culminates in addictions of various kinds, whether they manifest as: chemical addictions, food addictions, gambling addictions, sexual addictions, or other addictions. It makes no difference what the addiction is. It has the same root. It comes from the same place— no matter how it manifests or what triggers it— because it is all about trying to fill a lustful, craving apart from God. It is rooted in self- centeredness, "trying to make me happy, trying to make me feel good, and trying to make me feel better". All of these are perversions of God's proper design. God uses appropriate doctor prescribed medication to bring healing from time to time; but the devil uses drug addictions to take people out. Alcohol has its place according to Scripture; but the devil uses it to destroy lives and families. There are better ways to gain money than through gambling. Sex is for marriage only; people with sexual addictions end up with diseases. There are consequences for every action. Jesus said, "Count the cost!"

If we are going to be free of the issues that are hindering us and holding us back from being all God called us to be, we must come out of our self-centered attitudes and take responsibility for our lives. We must turn over our will, our intellect, and our emotions to Him; and we must stop allowing our soul to rule and control us. We must be led and directed by the spirit and surrender to His Spirit. If we say we are His, we must be like Him. We will not do this perfectly; but that cannot be our excuse for not doing it at all. At the end of the day, it is not about us. We cannot make it about us. If we make it about us, we are missing the big picture; and we are missing the purpose for which God has called us.

Some may not want to hear this message. They may try to shift the blame to make it about others so they do not have to take responsibility for their lives. Some do this in clever and subtle ways. I was doing this at the time my pastor's wife corrected me and inspired the writing of this book. No matter how smart we are, or think we are, we cannot outsmart the Holy Spirit. He searches the hearts of men. I was frustrated and angry. I was blaming everyone I could except for myself for my life at the time. I was not accepting any responsibility for anything that I was dealing with at that time; and even though there was plenty of blame to go around, I deserved to accept my fair share. She saw to it and ensured that I accepted my fair share. Shortly after that, things began to turn around for me.

When we refuse to accept responsibility for our lives, we will stay stuck in a place of pain. It took me a couple of years after I met her to begin to accept some responsibility. Once I did, I had to learn how much to accept and how much to reject because people will always try to put responsibility on you that isn't yours to take. They want to blame you for things you could not possibly have known or controlled. Unfortunately, there is a very true expression, "Hindsight is 20-20!" They forget they were just as deceived as you were by certain people and situations; and they want to blame you for not having foreknowledge of the events that were occurring, because they figured it out before you.

The key to victory in this process is to walk in the Spirit, like we are instructed in Galatians 5:16 and to stay out of the intellect and emotions. In Isaiah 55, we are told God does not think the way we do, His ways are higher than our ways and His thoughts are higher than our thoughts. According to The Word of God, our thoughts come from three sources or influences: the devil (see Genesis 3; and Matthew 4), our own lusts or evil desires (see James 1), and God (see Joel 2 and Acts 2). Often, we do not recognize the influence of our thoughts immediately; but we see them as we reflect on them over time and we see where they have led us. This is why it is critical that we are thinking in ways that honor and glorify Him. To do this, we must think like Him. If we are going to think like Him, we have to lay our thoughts aside, look to Him, and let Him put His thoughts in us, according to Colossians 3:1-3. We must be Kingdom-centered and Kingdom-focused.

Also, we cannot walk in our emotions because our emotions change based on circumstances. God is looking for stability and diligence from His people. Only those who are Kingdom-minded can be stable; these are the ones who are strong and secure in their faith, looking always to Christ regardless of what their circumstances are dictating, their emotions are screaming, or what makes sense to them or anybody else. They take responsibility for their lives and look to the Holy Spirit to help them get free from the issues in their hearts and lives. They seek His discernment for how much responsibility to accept when others attempt to shift blame to them. Where they may have been wrong, they make amends if they can, forgive themselves, and move on. When they were the victim of someone else's deception which resulted in faulty decisions they would not have otherwise made, and are blamed for those follow-up decisions, they forgive all parties involved including themselves and move on. When the perception of guilt is faulty and they are looked at as a scapegoat to place blame on making them a convenient target, they forgive the accuser because they recognize the accuser's spirit behind it.

No matter the situation, they learn to release it to the Lord and allow the Blood of Jesus to cover it– fixing whatever they cannot. They trust Him for healing and restoration where it is needed because He is The LORD, our Healer, and our Deliverer.

SECTION 2

"(Name or situation) is the Reason for All My Problems"

CHAPTER 4

"Help! I'm stuck!"

Children like to play "Dodge Ball", where the object is to avoid getting hit by the oncoming ball. If you get hit, you are out of the game. Another fun childhood game is "Hot Potato". In this game, the object is to pass the ball from person to person, without dropping it. These people are spaced apart. Whoever drops the ball is out of the game. Unfortunately, many people live as if they are still playing these childhood ball games—afraid to take responsibility for the issues in their lives. They avoid taking responsibility for their lives and pass the blame onto someone else. That is not to say that people don't have a profound impact and influence upon our lives; they do. 1 Corinthians 15:33 (NKJV) teaches that bad company corrupts good morals. Still, we must know where to set boundaries in our lives and take our problems before God, allowing Him to help us find solutions to everything hindering us. There is no problem that He cannot solve.

There are four primary ways in which we pass the blame to others, and each manifest differently. This chapter deals with staying stuck in the past. The next chapter focuses on playing the victim. The following chapter speaks to those who expect rejection and failure at every turn. The last four chapters in this section focus on those who live in fear and hopelessness, showing in particular how they manifest. The common element in all of these is the person who is stuck in any stage of this is deceiving himself or herself. The deceived person is under the illusion that he or she has made it about the person or situation they are blaming; but really, the person blamed has already moved on with their lives. The perceived victim is the one who is bound. That situation may have been a forerunner to a bunch of bad decisions, but it is not anything that God cannot undo. The only limits God has are the ones we place on Him through our doubt and unbelief (see Matthew 13:54-58). So take the limits off, and believe God for what He says belongs to you.

Looking in the spiritual realm, those who are stuck in the past resemble someone who is stuck in quicksand. You believe you are standing secure and firm. Suddenly without warning, it begins to suck you in little by little until you cannot move and cannot breathe. I have never experienced the physical manifestation; but there was a time that I was stuck in the past, as I testified earlier, and my pastor's wife had to help rescue me spiritually. It was a frightening place to be!

One of the biggest manifestations of being stuck in the past is un-forgiveness or bitterness. You may feel as if you have a right to hold onto your anger because of the way in which you were wronged. Others may support or defend your right to be angry. Nevertheless, if you hold onto that anger, it will do three things. First, it will eat you up inside. Second, it will turn you into a person you do not want to be and no one else wants to be around. Finally, it will separate you from God; and if you refuse to repent and forgive, it will cost you your salvation (see Matthew 6: 14-15). When you think you have a right to stay angry at someone for something they have done to you, the best way to convince yourself to forgive them is to ask yourself, "Are they worth losing my salvation over?" That always motivates me to forgive someone I'm not otherwise willing to forgive because my relationship with God is too valuable to me to lose. I will not "cast my pearls before swine" (see Matthew 7:6).

Another big manifestation of someone who is stuck in the past is someone who is stuck in guilt or shame. This is similar to un-forgiveness; but rather than the un-forgiveness being directed outward, it is directed inward. There is also a subtle difference between guilt and shame. Guilt is un-forgiveness towards oneself because of actions or attitudes. Shame is un-forgiveness towards yourself because you don't like who you are. For example: I might feel guilty for not saying goodbye to my pastor and his wife before I leave service on Sunday because I love them and they are my spiritual parents. I was raised that it is bad manners to leave a host's house without saying goodbye, especially if they are your parents. However, I would be ashamed of myself if I thought God had called me to be a doctor because I do not have a scientific mind. Praise God, I know better and I stay in my lane! That is not my call.

Un-forgiveness, bitterness, guilt, and shame lead to regrets which are other manifestations that someone is stuck in the past. Regrets also differ because they are long-lasting and because they are not based on what we have done or on whom we are or are not; but instead, they are based on what we have failed to accomplish. For example, many people regret the things they have never had the courage to try. There are many reasons for the failure to take risks. Some reasons include: fear of success, fear of failure, fear of rejection, confusion leading to indecision, and procrastination. The bottom line is if you never try, you never succeed; and you will never regret those things you accomplish. Other people regret things that they started but left unfinished for one reason or another. Many have regrets in each category.

So how do we overcome our past? It is a simple process; but it is not easy. If it was easy, everyone would do it; but nothing worthwhile is easy. The first thing to remember is God is not out to torment us. He would not tell us to do something that was not possible. The fact that He tells us to be overcomers (see Revelation 21:7) means we can be. Stop doubting! Press into God, get to know Him intimately and you will see we have the victory in Christ! (see 1 Corinthians 15: 55-58; and 1 John 5: 4-15).

Once we realize that we have the victory in Christ, we must choose to forgive anyone that we have not forgiven; and repent of our un-forgiveness. Repent of anything else you feel guilty for and forgive yourself. Lay any shame you have at the foot of the Cross. Ask the Holy Spirit to reveal who He created you to be because that is who you really are, not who you think you are or whom others think you are. Then, ask Him to help you to become who He created you to be. Surrender all your desires and ambitions, hopes and dreams to Him. Let Him put His desires in you. As He puts His desires in you, ask Him to reveal to you what He wants you to accomplish and in what timing; and trust Him to supply the resources and give you the words as you need them. Then, commit to walking in His will as He reveals it to you. When He says, "Move!" don't procrastinate; so doubt can't settle in. Hebrews 11:1 tells us that faith is now!

The process is simple; but it is painful. There is no way to avoid the pain. Author and conference speaker, Joyce Meyers is known for saying, "There's the pain of change; and there's the pain of staying the same." It is up to us to choose! This is the equivalent of going to wound management for treatment for a bad infection that is interfering with your walk. Spiritually, that is what it does. Dr. Jesus goes deep inside with his scalpel and digs out all the infected junk that is causing us so much pain. You cannot expect it to feel good to have a sharp object deep inside an infected open wound that is already sore; but it is a necessary process for healing. For those who choose the pain of change, there is healing from the inside-out and freedom.

Sadly, many choose not to do the work involved to come to this place of healing and freedom because they do not want to walk through the painful memories of their lives again to see them from God's perspective, nor do they want to look at themselves in the mirror honestly and allow the Holy Spirit to refine them because it hurts. What they don't realize is the pain they are attempting to avoid is temporary; but they are already tormented by the past. That past will settle in, become permanent, and destroy them unless they allow Jesus to set them free. Like the servant in the parable in Matthew 25 who wasted his talent, many continue blaming others for their own unhappiness instead of taking responsibility for their lives. They may even blame the One Who can lead them out and Who gave them their talents.

The most surefire way to waste your life and your talents are to stay stuck in the past. The Lord tells His people to: "Forget those things that lay behind and press on toward the mark of the high calling of God in Christ Jesus" (see Philippians 4:13). What does that mean exactly and how does that tie in with the caution that those who forget where they came from are doomed to repeat the past? Here's how this works. We seek God for the lessons He wants us to learn from our experiences and those of others. What can we gain from our lives and the testimony of others? Then, we take that insight and wisdom and store it up until the Holy Spirit gives us an application; and we are free to put the past behind us because the past has served its purpose. If we stay stuck in the past beyond that, it has outlived its usefulness.

Another way people stay stuck in the past is when they refuse to learn the lessons that God has called them to; so they repeat the same issues. The Old Testament is filled with examples of this. The Israelites who were God's Covenant people were constantly in and out of bondage to their enemies because of their rebellion. Their rebellion was influenced by illegal covenants they made with foreign nations who were serving other gods. While in bondage to these foreign nations, some of these monarchs took great care of Israel because the LORD was watching over them in His mercy. Other monarchs abused Israel horribly so that the LORD could pour out the full weight of His judgment upon the nations rebelling against Him. Even in the midst of the worst persecution, God still looked out for His people. When things were good Israel celebrated and praised the Lord, giving Him honor and glory; but frequently, when they were in pain, they complained and turned to idols. Because of this trend, He stopped an entire generation from going into the Promised Land (see Numbers chapters 13-14). Their doubt and unbelief kept them out and kept them stuck in the past!

Those who understand that our lives are neither about us nor about the others around us want to be free. They want to do whatever it takes to become whom God has called them to be because they understand that what matters most is where they stand in their relationship with Him. If that isn't right, nothing else matters. They will walk through the pain of change and they will help others come into that place of healing and freedom in Christ because they don't want to waste the talents God gave them. They don't have time to play the blame game anymore because their time has become too valuable and it's become too important to them that God uses them. They know they can't be effective if they avoid taking responsibility for their lives, simply because it hurts.

CHAPTER 5

"Get out of Your Victim's Mentality!"

quote in the "Inspirational Video" section entitled "Dare to Be Great" of the *Think Positive* series that I was receiving by email in 2014 says, "We are all meant to shine as children. As we give ourselves permission to shine, we unconsciously liberate others." Scripture supports this. God created us in freedom. He made Adam and Eve, first as spiritual beings. Then, He clothed them in flesh and set them in a garden– surrounded by all the beauty of nature. He told them they could eat of any tree they wanted except for one because it would kill them; but the devil deceived Eve and they went after the tree they were told not to eat, putting all of creation in bondage (see Genesis chapters 1-3). Jesus came to set the captives free; but only those who choose to receive His free gift of eternal life can walk in true liberty (see John 10:10). It's our job to shine the light of Christ so others can be free as well (see Matthew 5:14-16). This is the message of the Gospel.

This isn't an unconscious choice, but a conscious one. However, many choose darkness rather than light (see John 3:14-21), or they decide not to choose. Ironically their decision is a choice. What most do not realize, as the video points out, is "It is our light, not our darkness that most frightens us." I neither believed this nor understood it, when I first heard it. I had to hear it several times before its truth sank in. The reality is we become overwhelmed by the amount of potential that God has put in us until we learn to seek direction from the Holy Spirit and allow Him to focus it. Once He focuses you, you discover what you're worth and you can go out and get what you're worth, like Sylvester Stallone advises.

Going out and getting what you're worth does not come without its challenges. I learned long ago, nothing worthwhile comes easy. I also learned that winners never quit and quitters never win! I can be hard on myself, particularly with setbacks and failures; however I have improved greatly. It used to give me a defeatist attitude, which depressed me for days; but I always picked myself up, dusted myself off, and kept going. Lately, I pick myself up much quicker, usually within a few hours.

One thing my pastor's wife said that helped me was, "We don't make mistakes; we make discoveries. When you make a mistake, you just discovered that it was something that didn't work, so you try something else." That is so freeing! When I heard in the "Inspirational Video" section entitled *Overcoming Adversity* of the *Think Positive* series, "With each failure, you are that much closer to your inevitable victory" and "You will make the impossible, possible!" I was prepared to receive that. Unfortunately, many who have come to expect failure and rejection have a victim's mentality. For years, I was one of them.

People with a victim's mentality expect people to mistreat them and put them down in every situation they encounter. For example, my church begins our service on Sunday mornings with spiritual declarations that come straight out of the Word of God. One of these is "I am the head and not the tail, above only and not beneath" (see Deut. 28). When I first joined my church years ago, I had difficulty saying that declaration. My mentality was. "I don't want to be under anybody's feet because I don't need to be stepped on, but I don't need to be on top either because people are always trying to knock off the head. I'm perfectly content to have God put me somewhere in the middle where I can be safe and pray for those who are above me. I don't need the responsibility; and I don't want to worry about messing up, being sabotaged, or having my character assassinated. Thank you very much" (attitude should be included for the right effect). It took me a long time to understand that the high place was a place of honor and respect, not a place of punishment, that God did not put someone in that office because no one else was willing to do it, and that He was not looking to punish or assassinate someone.

My wrong concepts came through watching my dad who owned a small business (from my earliest memory) lose his company to his colleague's son when I was in my early twenties. It nearly bankrupted him financially, but it hurt his heart emotionally. This had a lasting impact on me. I also saw this supported in Scripture through the many monarchs that were killed off by God and men; and when David killed Goliath after he threw the stone, he brought the head back to King Saul as a trophy (see 1 Samuel 17). John the Baptist's head was delivered to some girl's mother in a charger (see Matt. 14:1-10; and Mark 6:14-28). It didn't take me long to see a connection, even if it was wrong.

The problems I had with my relationship with my mom added to my confusion. God used my church to restore the headship to its rightful place of honor in my life and in my heart. Once He restored this, I was able to treat my leadership with the respect and honor they deserve; and I was able to say that declaration without any attitude and without regrets.

One of the big problems I had with leadership, spiritual or otherwise, was I expected them to manipulate and control me. Therefore, I had problems with submission when I first came to my church. I didn't see this back then because I said in my heart, "I'm open to suggestions; I just don't want anyone telling me what to do." That isn't Biblical. I wanted to appear submissive because I wanted to obey God, but my heart was not submissive. I questioned anything and everything that did not make sense to me. I was trapped in my intellect. A lot of it was a control issue. I was fighting for control. I didn't trust my leaders yet; so, I felt like I had to figure everything out. It was my safety net. The Holy Spirit showed me this much later. I saw rules and discipline as a form of control, so I particularly questioned any rule I did not understand. Victims expect leaders to use rules to control and manipulate, and see consequences as bondage.

In the last several years, I've come to understand the purpose of rules, discipline, and consequences. These boundaries provide the protection and guidance that keep us safe from danger. Loving leaders make the right choices simple, even when they are not easy. There is a difference between something being simple and easy. If it is simple, it is clear and obvious; it is practical, but walking it out might still be a long, emotional battle. Things that are easy come naturally, whether or not they are the right thing to do in a given situation. I praise God for leaders who have taught me that decisions can be simple, even when they are not easy; and that God will empower me to walk through even those emotionally turbulent ones.

Having come through a lot of verbal abuse and insults, I never took criticism well. I recognized a pattern in 2014 and began to deal with it before God. I saw that when someone criticizes me, it really got inside me. It stayed with me for days, depending on the person, maybe longer. If I thought it was warranted, I might make whatever changes were necessary; but I got really down on myself, sometimes downright insulting or verbally abusive. If I didn't think it was warranted, I would get defensive trying to convince the other person that they're wrong. If they were someone I cared about or if it was something I could ignore, I tried to let it go. Because I came from an environment where you were presumed guilty until proven innocent survival required defending yourself before accusations surfaced. This meant that you had to be either extremely prophetic or a mind reader to survive; being defensive and becoming angry were more common responses for me.

Fortunately, I did a lot of yelling; and then cooled down, resulting in a lot of regrets. I never lashed out physically or destroyed things. Those are victim behaviors also. A person who does not have a victim's mindset is not so insecure. He or she can allow criticism to roll off his or her back without it wrecking his day, his week, etc.

My insecurities were severe enough that they pushed me inside myself but God has been gracious to me. I withdrew and shut down emotionally so that you couldn't get me to talk about what was bothering me; I avoided it. Instead I would talk about everything else. Few people could even tell something was on my mind because I was too good at hiding it. I hid in crowds. I would smile, laugh, and act natural; but if I wanted to hide you would never know something wasn't right. That's why I have made myself accountable to the senior members of my prayer team. They are all spiritual leaders, whether in their church or in mine; and I have known them for a minimum of four or five years. Most, I have known longer. Then, there are other members of my prayer team, who are not senior members; but they are equally important. I also confide in them from time to time. They are also spiritual leaders. Nevertheless, my senior members know me best. They are my first line of defense in a crisis. When I need prayer and spiritual reinforcements, after I have prayed through, I go to them first.

In the "Inspirational Video" section entitled *Overcoming Adversity* of the *Think Positive* series, Dustin Hughes encourages us, "This is your defining moment: be determined to be focused. Be relentless. Be intentional... Be unstoppable, be thankful, be in this moment... Live your passion, live your purpose, live your dreams." So how do we come out of our victim's mentality? The first thing we have to do is make a decision to see change in our lives. Someone once said, "Insanity is doing the same thing over and over while expecting different results." In the "Inspirational Video" section entitled *Winning is a Habit* of the *Think Positive* series, some challenging points are made. It is said, "The only question to ask yourself is: How much are you willing to give to achieve what you want? Most people know exactly what they want and what measures are necessary to get there. Until you start believing in yourself, you ain't going to have a life. Winning is not a sometimes thing. It's an all-the-time thing. You don't do things right once in a while. You do things right all the time. Winning is a habit! Make it yours too."

Jesus spoke of counting the costs (see Luke 14: 26- 33). It is our insecurities that hold us back and keep us from achieving our dreams. We judge ourselves unfairly. Brian G. Jett, in the "Inspirational Video" section, entitled *What They Don't Say* of the *Think Positive* series says: "You can determine how confident people are by listening to what they don't say about themselves." I had difficulty grasping what he meant by that at first. Then, something my pastor's wife said helped. She said that you can tell how spiritually mature someone is by what they talk about and what they don't talk about. She said, "When you're on the floor, all you see are dirt and bugs. The higher up you go in God, the more beauty you see. The dirt and the bugs no longer bother you as much" (see Colossians 3:1-4). That made sense to me. You deal with them; but they don't wreck your world and become a part of your conversation. It was a great perspective!

Victims are so torn down by the criticisms of others, either real or perceived, that they cannot get past it to pursue the dreams God has given them. One negative comment shuts them down because they have a thousand plus negative voices playing repeatedly like an endless tape recorder in their head. They think their dreams are overrated. They think everyone else is better than them. They think they deserve the short end of every double standard. In one of the *Think Positive* series, Courtney Hickman says: "A dream only becomes overrated when not pursued by the dreamer." Therefore, we need to forget what the naysayers have told us and listen to what God is speaking to us and about us because He is the One Who created us. He knows the potential He has put in us. He knows what He designed and created us for. He knows how to bring out our best and to maximize our potential.

Zig Ziglar, in the "Inspirational Video" section entitled *Attitude Makes All the Difference* of the *Think Positive* series, tells us two things that are critical for changing our destiny. He says, "Negative self-talk can destroy your ability to have the life you want." That is what is meant by Proverbs 18: 21. If you speak negative things, negative things will keep occurring; but you can turn that around by speaking God's Word over your life and your situation. The other thing pertains to all those people that we hold responsible for the problems in our lives and want to change. He says, "You'll never change them until you change you." My pastor's wife puts it this way, "People are not your problem. You are." Why is that? It is because usually what bothers us most about them is stuff we have not faced in us.

CHAPTER 6

"Who Called You A Failure?"

Those with a victim's mentality know the worst aspects are: feelings of failure, fear of more failure, and fear of rejection. After all, most of us were raised to believe that people don't want to be around failures; everyone loves a winner. We are inspired by the underdog who suddenly has a comeback victory; but if someone doesn't like you, they label you a "Loser!" It's meant to be derogatory. No wonder people fear failure and rejection! Those who have been made to feel like victims their whole lives experience these feelings to a greater degree.

Some of the ways they express their fear of failure can be more subtle than others. Some people who are afraid of failure are downright stubborn and prideful. They cannot and will not admit they are wrong, even when it is obvious to them and everyone else, because they are afraid of looking foolish. I'm not that person. I may be stubborn sometimes, making me slow to pick up on things when I'm wrong; but I eventually get it, and when I'm wrong, I say I'm wrong. My problem is more subtle.

I didn't know I was doing this until the Holy Spirit opened my eyes.I've dealt with my fear of failure in one of two ways depending on what I was facing. If God asks me to do something that I wasn't sure how to do, I would fall back on something that seemed similar to it that I had previously done. It never entered my mind that God could be moving differently. If I was taking an even bigger risk and doing something I didn't have a frame of reference for; I'd try to copy someone I admired expecting the same results without considering that their personal journey with the Lord may be different and influence the results. I did this because I was afraid of failure and looking foolish. The end result was that because I got ahead of God or completely bypassed His direction, I fell on my face and ended up looking foolish anyway.

Some, who fall on their face after doing everything they know to do, want to go back and blame everyone who gave them advice for it not working, or they blame God. However, they probably didn't take time to seek God, or if they did, they probably didn't wait for an answer. If they waited for an answer they decided that their way was better; and it blew up in their face. That is not God's fault! We are not failures. God did not create us to be failures; but our efforts apart from Him are (see John 15: 1- 11). We will never have any lasting success apart from Him. He may allow us to taste a little bit of success to keep us encouraged, to let us know that He has not forsaken nor abandoned us. Those who do not discern that properly can misread these signals and go out of position.

Reacting to the fear of failure, many with the victim's mentality express their fear of rejection in different ways. Some lash out to keep from being hurt by others. This can be done verbally or physically. Others withdraw inside themselves. The more complex people use a mixture of these approaches. The problem is these behaviors only breed more rejection. We must break the cycle and there is a way to do it! God promises freedom to those who are willing to receive it.

Like coming out of any bondage the devil has deceived us into setting up for ourselves, we must choose to get free. This often starts with believing that we can be. We must stop believing the lies the devil tells us about ourselves, we tell ourselves, and those other people have told us about ourselves. Are they greater than the God who created us? The God of the Universe cared so much about us that He took the time to create us in a two-step process. First, He created us as spirit beings in Genesis chapter 1. Then, in Genesis chapter 2, He formed us in His image and likeness out of the dust of the ground. He formed us carefully, crafting all the little details about us: making sure that each nose and eye was exactly the right shape for the right face (see Psalm 119:73; and Psalm 139: 1-18). He is into details. He formed us out of the dust of the ground because all the wealth of the earth comes from the ground: diamonds, gold, silver, and precious stones. Even our

American money is made from paper and coins which come from trees and various metals. We were made to be prosperous and very rich. If we are not, we are living below the purpose for which God created us. We are not failures.

We become prosperous as we first pursue Him and have a Kingdom mindset. Jesus said in Matt. 6:33 "Seek ye first the Kingdom of God and His righteousness; and all these things shall be added unto you." What will God give to someone who will not deny Him anything? He will give him everything. The problem is most people want God to give them everything; but they do not want to give up anything. God is merciful and gracious with those who are new believers; but after a while, He expects His children to grow up and be willing to bring something to the table. He gave us everything. Why are we so reluctant? He did not even spare His only Son for us (see Romans 8:32). Doesn't He deserve our best? The Kingdom is about ministry and service to God first, then to His people, and then to others.

He made us in His image and likeness, but only the ones who fellowship with Him continually will become like Him (see Psalm 115). That's why it is critical we are mindful of what we allow to consume us. Those are the things that we worship. We were created for fellowship with Him. Fellowship is more than just socializing with someone. It's intimacy, it's transparency, and it's sacrificial. It is about being real with them. It won't allow you to stay stuck in the past; it makes you progress forward, to discover new things about yourself and about each other. If you're stuck in the past and not relating to each other in new ways, then you are not experiencing true fellowship. If there is fear in the relationship instead of a healthy respect, there is no fellowship. If you can't be transparent with each other and share your heart openly without fear of rejection or misunderstanding, there is no fellowship. You are only socializing. God created us to fellowship with Him and with each other. That's why rejection hurts so much. Romans 8:32 also proves that we're not rejected.

After we stop listening to the lies that keep playing like a tape recorder repeatedly in our heads, we must choose to forgive those who have hurt us. They didn't know the greatness God put in us. They didn't have God's perspective so they couldn't see it. If your perspective is off, your vision isn't going to be clear. We need to understand that they were responding out of the pain in their own heart. "Hurting people hurt people," as the expression goes; it's true. If their criticism is legitimate, then ask God for help in changing it and let yourself off the hook. If it is a bunch of hot air, take it with a grain of salt and let it roll off your back. Just hit the delete button and act like you never heard it.

Jesus gave us a clear warning. He told us that if you get rid of something that's not working, you need to replace it with something that works. Otherwise, something worse may move in to take its place (see Matthew 12: 43-45; and Luke 11: 24-26). So what should you fill it with? Some people try to fill it with philosophy or psychology, or other things that sound good. Some of these have some benefits for a time, but they all have spirits attached to them. Only one thing is guaranteed to work in every situation: The Word of God. The prophet Isaiah wrote: "The grass withers and the flower fades; but The WORD of God stands forever" (see Isaiah 40:8).

King David, the greatest Old Testament king Israel had called The Word of God a "lamp unto his feet and a light unto his path" (see Psalm 119:105). Earlier in Psalm 119, David says, "Wherewithal shall a young man cleanse his way? By taking heed thereto according to Thy Word. With my whole heart have I sought thee: O let me not wander from Thy Commandments. Thy Word have I hid in mine heart that I might not sin against Thee. Blessed art Thou, O LORD: teach me Thy Statutes" (see verses 9-12). David valued the Word so much that he hid it in his heart and used it as a guide for every decision he made. He cried out to God for a deeper understanding of His Word so that he would not fall into deception and make the wrong decisions. That's how important it must be to us and even more. It must consume our thoughts because our words reveal what we're thinking about, whether or not we're conscious of them (see Ecclesiastes 10:20; Matthew 15:1-20; and Mark 7:1-23). God activated this principle for us by speaking all of creation into existence for us (see Hebrews 11) and He gives His children who are in a covenant relationship with Him the same authority (see Pr. 18:21; and Romans 4:8-25).

We must apply the right word, to the right situation. That's why we need the Holy Spirit and we need solid Biblical teaching. Hebrews 10 instructs us not to forsake the assembling of ourselves together in Christian fellowship, as some are in the habit of doing. This is a touchy subject for some; but it must be addressed because God deals with it. Some make the excuse that they don't want to be in church because there are too many hypocrites in The Church. That excuse is hypocritical because it's saying that they're too good for the Body of Christ whom Jesus shed His Blood for and has chosen as His Bride (see Revelation 21). Are there hypocrites in The Church? Of course, there are. There's also, many honest people who are trying to live out what they believe the best they can and being wrongly accused and judged for making very big and public mistakes in their humanity.

God redeems and restores even the broken places of our lives that we give to Him, even when we cause the brokenness. He forgives us when we truly repent and He doesn't hold it against us any longer. He does not reject us and no one else has the right to hold our past against us, once we give it to Him. "Get the log out of your own eye. Then, you can see clearly to help your brother" (see Matthew 7:1-5).

Another excuse they give is that all the church wants is your money. First of all, if you want to get technical about it, we are not giving it to the church. We are giving to God. When you pay your bill to the electric company, do you see the person who receives your check? No you don't, nor do you question that it's being used correctly. You see the benefits from the money you turn in every time you turn on the light switch and you can see. Our church leaders are God's Kingdom agents who provide us the spiritual nourishment from The Word of God to help us grow. If they are not helping you grow spiritually, even if that growth is uncomfortable at times, find another church. If they're helping you grow spiritually, don't be reluctant to give. They're God's Kingdom agents who are serving Him.

Secondly, they have bills to pay too in order to provide a building for you to come and have services to worship God in. If you honor the leaders that God has called you to, and you need to, then do not complain about sowing financially. Honor begets honor. Finally, and most importantly, tithes and offerings were not their idea. They were God's idea (see Malachi 3: 1-12). You cannot reap if you do not sow anything (see Galatians 6:7). God built that principle into the universe to prosper you, not to break you. So, get planted and sow your seed.

In addition to these things, make yourself accountable to your leadership and fellowship with other fellow believers. Accountability is vital. It will help keep you on track, as nothing else will. Being accountable requires transparency. That means there can be no secrets from those who are holding you accountable. That is why I have a prayer team. It is not wise to have that level of transparency with everyone; you can't make yourself accountable to everyone. Some aren't trustworthy. Also, not everyone has God's heart for your situation. You need people who will hear from God. My pastor's wife teaches on this in-depth. They must also be ministry-minded and Kingdom-focused. You have to be willing to hold me accountable for the issues in my life.

Finally, stay diligent and consistent. If this seems like a lot, remember you didn't become a victim overnight; it's going to be a fight to get free. The devil does not want you free. Just remember, "We do not wrestle against flesh and blood; but against principalities and powers, against the rulers of the darkness of this world, and against spiritual wickedness in high places" (see Ephesians 6:12). Get your armor on (Ephesians 6:10-18). Take every thought into captivity to the obedience of Christ (see 2 Corinthians 4:3-6). Keep your eyes fixed on Christ (see Colossians 3:1-3). Be Kingdom- focused and ministry-minded; and don't let the devil get the best of you— ever! You are not a failure! You are not rejected! You are an overcomer in Christ (see Romans 8: 33-39)!

CHAPTER 7

"Fear and Hopelessness Are Over!"

It finally happened. You hit rock bottom. It doesn't matter what it took to get you there. Everyone has a different bottom. What matters is that you have been broken and humbled. You have come to a place where everything in your life is dead or dying. Nothing you try is working anymore. You are afraid all the time. You don't want to die; but you don't see any other way out. All you want is for the pain to be over. You are tired of running and you have run out of places to hide. You do not know what to do. You feel lost, hopeless, and confused. You feel like giving up. Don't give up! God has allowed you to come to a place of self-examination. What you choose to do now will determine how well you come out of this. You don't have to stay stuck! You can get free!

This journey will take a lot of prayer, reliance upon God, transparency, and accountability. You must be willing to fight as you have never fought before because you're fighting for your survival. Find your song because it will help get you through those tough times, even if you can't sing it in the right spirit initially. Your song will be one that you can relate to, but also encourages you. Whether you are celebrating or doing spiritual warfare, praise and worship work because praise tears down the walls and ushers in the Presence of God. That is why the priests carrying the Ark of the LORD always went before the LORD's army when Israel went out to fight. This standard was set when they took over the land of Canaan in the book of Joshua. God doesn't mind dealing with raw emotions as long as He has your heart.

There are other reasons why you want to continue to praise the Lord in spite of what you're going through. "The joy of the LORD is your strength" (see Nehemiah 8:10). "A merry heart does good like a medicine; but a broken spirit drieth the bones," (see Proverbs 17:22). That means if you find ways to enjoy your life, you can become healthier; but if you stay in a state of negativity, you will continue to make yourself ill. Furthermore, He strengthens those who put their trust in Him and there is no greater way to prove that you trust Him than to praise and worship Him when your world appears to be falling down around you. Those who love Him will want to obey Him. He loves us so much that He wants us to celebrate Him. He not only commands us to praise and worship Him; but He also commands us to enjoy it. Read Psalm chapters 146-150; and (one of my favorites on this topic) 1 Chronicles 16:23-36, which is repeated in Psalm chapter 29. Finally, you will not have a better reason than this: He is worthy!

If you are having trouble finding something to praise and worship God for, start with your salvation. If you have not yet given your life to Jesus Christ, I have included a simple prayer at the end of this book so that you have an opportunity to do that. He loved you too much to live without you. So, I urge you; do not leave this earth without Him. The greatest gift you will ever receive is JESUS! Beyond your salvation, you can thank Him for your life because there are many who did not wake up; and if you are alive and you are not happy with your life right now, you still have the opportunity to make the decisions needed to change it. You do not have to stay stuck. You can thank Him for creating the beautiful world around you. Even if it is cloudy and gloomy outside, rain brings refreshing and helps make the vegetation grow. There is always something to praise God for.

In addition to staying in praise and worship; stay in The Word. It is the Weapon by which you will fight off the attacks of the enemy. Even Jesus, when He was tempted said, "It is written…" (see Matt. 4:1-11; and Luke 4:1- 14). If it was good enough for Him, it should be good enough for us. Remember, our enemy is not a physical enemy; he is a spiritual one. So, God gave us spiritual weapons to counter them. We only have four offensive weapons: praise, worship, prayer, and the Word of God (see Ephesians 6). All the others: the helmet of salvation, the breastplate of the righteousness of God, the shield of faith, the belt of truth, and the preparation of the Gospel of peace are defensive. This tells me God will be doing our fighting for us; all we have to do is stand still and see His salvation (see also Exodus 14:13); and even when we have a part to play in a battle, God has well equipped us. Because He has equipped us so well and He made the universe– including our adversary–, we don't have to be afraid. All we have to do is stay in the Presence of the Lord because "where the Spirit of the Lord is, there is liberty" (see 2 Corinthians 3:17). God is love and there is no fear in love because fear has torment, so he who fears is not made perfect in love, according to 1 John 4. I walk on eggshells each time I am around certain individuals, afraid of making them angry; so, it interferes with my ability to express the kind of love I have for them in my heart. It hurts me. However, when I am in the Presence of God, I am not afraid of them.

Because of the freedom that the Holy Spirit wants to give us and because He loves us so much, He wants us to live and dwell in His Presence. That's what Psalm 91 is all about. When we spend time dwelling in His shadow, we become like Him and He takes care of us. Then, we have nothing to fear. All our needs get met and no one can harm us. All we have to do is magnify Him and exalt Him, which means to make Him bigger and lift Him up (see Psalm 34:3).Think of a telescope.

What are we making Him bigger than? We are enlarging Him over our problems and situations that seem larger than us. What are we lifting Him up over? We are lifting Him up over everything that is dragging us down. He can handle it. He is bigger than all of it. Give it to Him and leave it with Him. When we spend our quality time with Him, He restores our soul (see Psalm 23). Our soul is different than our spirit. Our soul is the seat bed of our mind. It contains our will, intellect, and emotions. When the Lord asks for our heart, He wants us to give Him our soul. Peace and freedom come in the surrender.

We must also have spiritual accountability. Therefore, we must stay connected to our spiritual leaders within our home church and others whom we have chosen to be accountable to. When we are going through hard times, isolation is so dangerous. We must be transparent and let others we trust know our needs so they can provide the appropriate support and prayer. Ecclesiastes 4:8-10 supports this. Do not isolate yourself physically or emotionally in a crisis. Continue being transparent and stay accountable, or you will wish you did. If your leaders give you advice, follow it. It is for your benefit.

Do not be afraid to ask for help and do not allow anyone to make you feel ashamed for needing it. I was taught from an early age that it was not safe to share your personal business outside of family. So, I learned to stay silent about my problems. When things got so bad that I finally started talking, I was not believed because who is going to believe a teenager over an upstanding professional in the community when all the physical evidence is hidden? So, I learned to shut down emotionally and take my emotions out on my vehicle, because I knew that my car would not accuse me of lying when I was telling the truth. I needed rescuing and I could not get anyone to listen. Meanwhile, I was made to feel ashamed for needing help– no matter who was at fault. I have since learned that there is no shame in needing help. The only shame is in needing help and not getting it. If you need help, get it.

This help may come in the form of psychological or other counseling. Just ensure that the counselor you work with is a practicing Christian who uses Biblical principles, whether or not they work in a Christian agency. The Lord hides His richest treasures in the darkest places sometimes, so be open to hearing the Holy Spirit. Ask your pastor or a member of your church staff for a referral if you need this. God can do tremendous inner healing in a person's life for those who are open to receive this type of ministry. Unfortunately, when my pastor's wife referred me to a friend of hers, I was not yet ready. I was too ashamed to ask for the help I needed. It was embarrassing to me, and I had allowed my shame to stand in the way of the healing God wanted to bring into my life. I also had a tremendous fear of authority; and when I became angry with them, I was so intimidated by them, I could not express it. Intimidation was a significant stronghold in my life. When my pastor's wife gave me her referral, I knew she had my best interest at heart, and I knew how much she loved me. So, I consented to try it, for her– not for me. If you are in counseling for anyone other than you, even someone you love and respect, it will not work. It has to be something the Holy Spirit puts on your heart to do. I went for a while, but because of where I was at, it didn't work.

My counselor gave me a writing assignment that I put my heart and soul into. It took a couple weeks to complete. Writing is my passion. If you give me a writing assignment, feel free to give me an honest opinion and critique after reading my work; but do not ask me to write something for you, refuse to read it, and then criticize something you have never read. To me, that is the equivalent of throwing it into the trash can. That is what this woman did.

First, she told me it was too long without giving me a word count or a page count. Then, because many of our counseling sessions had centered around my mom, she assumed I had spent multiple pages writing about my mom when very little of it had anything to do with her because it was not relevant to the assignment. I am professional when I write. When given an assignment, I stick to the assignment. I was furious; but was too intimidated by her authority to tell her. Therefore, I stopped attending. God later set me free of my fear of authority figures; and when I saw her again, I was with my mom and daughter in the mall. It took me a while to remember who she was, after we parted ways. Once I remembered her, I realized why I felt awkward around her. I had unfinished business with her. I never had the opportunity to tell her that I forgave her and to ask for her forgiveness for how poorly I had handled the situation. It took me a while to see that I still needed help and get it. Once I sought the help I needed for the right reasons, I made wonderful progress.

Know that the fear and the hopelessness are over! God is on your side! "If God be for us who can be against us?" (see Romans 8:31). "For God has not given us a spirit of fear; but of power, of love, and of a sound mind" (see 2 Timothy 1:7). Whom shall I fear? There is nothing man can do to me God cannot stop. If He allows it, it is for my benefit. So, I may as well see what He is trying to teach me through it. Then, I can move on. He has promised to work all things for the good of those who love Him and are called according to His purpose (see Romans 8:28). That does not mean everything is good initially. It means that He brings good out of it, but there are prerequisites.

First, we must be passionately in love with Him and walking in His plans and purposes to see that manifest in our lives. Finally, He has an innumerable company of angels ready to help us as soon as they hear His Word released into the atmosphere (see 2 Kings 6:8-23; and Psalm 103:19- 22). A believer in right standing with God may go through their seasons of blessing and hardships (see Ecclesiastes 3); but their life is never hopeless.

CHAPTER 8

"Driven to Deception"

Children love wearing masks. That is one reason that Halloween is popular with them. They have vivid imaginations and can make up anything. Some of the tales they can create can make your hairs stand up on end. It is often fun to watch and it has its place; but at some point, we are supposed to outgrow this– at least to some extent. The Word of God tells us "to put away childish things" (see 1 Corinthians 13:11). This doesn't mean that good acting cannot be used appropriately as a form of entertainment because God gives creative gifts to bless His children, to minister to others, to spread His message, and to bring Him glory. Nevertheless, many end up with twisted thinking and are driven to deception because of fear and intimidation. This is a dangerous place to be.

An example of this that we see in Scripture comes from Genesis. It comes from the story of Jacob and Essau. Many within the Body of Christ are familiar with this story. In Genesis 25:21-26, we see that God gave the mother of the boys (Rebekah) a prophecy at the time of their conception concerning the twins' future outcomes; but she was not totally willing to trust God to bring it to pass. She thought she had to help it along. How many of us are guilty of that? She played favorites. Isaac favored Essau, who was the first-born by minutes, while she favored Jacob.

When Essau returned from hunting, Jacob took venison and lentils and made them into a stew to entice his starving brother. Then, Jacob told Essau he could only have some if he sold his birthright over to

Jacob. Essau made a decision with eternal consequences based upon temporary emotions. Many of us do this too frequently also. Because he was so hungry, Essau became overly dramatic. He claimed he was starving to death and sold Jacob his birthright because it was more convenient to eat what was right in front of him than to go back out hunting. When the agreement was reached, Jacob fed him.

Once Isaac became blind in Genesis 27, Rebekah (the mother) overheard her husband's instructions to Essau, whom he favored for his hunting abilities. She devised a plan with Jacob to deceive Isaac into receiving the blessing of the first-born. She instructed him to put on Essau's clothing and cook up some of the meat they had stored up in reserve from Essau's previous hunting trips, and serve it to Isaac. Then, if questioned, Jacob should say, "God sent the animal to him quickly." The plan worked because of Jacob's charm and charisma; and because God had previously prophesied that He had a plan to bless Jacob over Essau. If God had not planned to bless Jacob, no amount of charm and charisma would have been enough. Nevertheless, because Rebekah did not trust God to fulfill His Word, she devised the plan; and because Jacob did not trust Him, he went along with it. This resulted in Jacob running for his life from his brother for several years.

When Jacob was running for his life, God had to cleanse Jacob of his deception by showing him— himself. Deception has many motives behind it. Some want to prove something to others. They have a spirit of superiority or arrogance. Some are afraid of what will happen if they do not fit into the mold others have created for them. Some want to get revenge for a wrong or a perceived wrong committed. Some are simply bored and are looking to stir up trouble as a form of amusement or entertainment. Behind nearly all of these various motives is fear. There are even those so bound by deception that they do not know how bound they are. This is the most tragic of all. How does this happen; and how does one get free after arriving at this place? What can occur if they don't allow God to deal with them?

Someone who is constantly changing their identity to fit into cultural expectations, and never get to know who they are as people often find themselves trapped in a spirit of deception. They are so busy going from one mask to another mask that they never have the opportunity to find out who God created them to be or what God has called them to do. They stuff their negative emotions so deep down inside them that they become almost incapable of feeling anything short of bitterness or rage after a while. I was trapped in this bondage for years; and it took the ministry of my best friend and her family to prepare me for the ministry of my church, which God has used to show me who I am in Christ.

In Jacob's case, God used Laban, who was his maternal uncle, to show Jacob the deception inside his heart. In Genesis 28, Jacob was sent to Laban to take a bride from among Laban's daughters; and he had to work for Laban to win the right to marry the bride of his choice. In working for Laban, he found that Laban was not forthcoming with him. Jacob fell in love with Rachel in Genesis 29. Instead of giving Rachel to Jacob in marriage right away as agreed upon, he gave Leah to him first. Jacob worked for Rachel for seven years. Making matters worse, Laban had Leah walk down the aisle in a wedding dress and veil. Jacob expected Rachel; but when Jacob raised the veil to kiss Rachel, he was surprised to find Leah there instead. It was a dirty trick. Laban's only explanation was, "I couldn't marry off the younger daughter before I marry off the older one; but if you want to marry Rachel, no problem. Just work for me another seven years." Jacob loved Rachel so much he agreed to it.

At the end of the second seven year period, he thought his time with Laban was done; but Laban had seen how everything he had prospered because of Jacob. When God decides to prosper you, he causes everything you touch to prosper; and everyone connected to you benefits because of it. Those who stand in your way and bring harm to you end up cursing themselves. You cannot curse what God has blessed; and you don't mess with God and His children, because He does not play! (See Psalm 5: 12).

After Jacob married Leah and Rachel, Laban saw the prosperity that came about into his life because of Jacob; and he thought to himself, "I've got to keep this going." As Jacob tended to Laban's flocks, he was told, "I'll give you all the speckled and spotted ones." Those were supposed to be the weaker ones; but God saw what Laban attempted to do. Laban was trying to make it appear like he was providing for Jacob and his family while trying to keep them dependent upon him rather than upon God. So, God made sure that the speckled and spotted cattle came out stronger. When Laban saw this, he switched it. As he switched it, God restored the ordinary cattle's strength; and the speckled and spotted ones came out weaker. Then, Laban accused Jacob of deception. Jacob's response was, "Excuse me! You're the one who keeps changing my wages." God was using Laban as a mirror to Jacob to show him the deception He was dealing with inside Jacob. At that point, they made a covenant recorded in Genesis 31:44-54.

Dealing with Laban became the turning point to change Jacob. Then, in Genesis 32:22-31, we read about the one event that put the capstone on it. It is so significant that Jacob's name changed, along with his character. When Jacob had tricked his father into giving him the blessing that legally belonged to Essau and Essau tried to get it from Isaac, Essau made a profound statement. Essau asked, "Is he not rightly named 'Jacob' because he is a deceiver for, he has twice deceived me: once out of my birthright and now out of my blessing?" Here in Genesis 32, Jacob is still on the run from Essau; Jacob and Laban have formed a covenant, so he has stopped running from Laban. Now, Jacob is crying out to God with his family whom God has blessed him with. He is tired of running. He wants to be free. He bottomed out. Are you there?

When Jacob reached that point, God gave him a dream. He saw a stairway to Heaven with angels on the stairs ascending and descending. He stopped one of them on the ascent back up the ladder. The angel said, "Let me go for the day breaks." Jacob replied, "I will not let you go unless you bless me." He wrestled with the angel until the angel finally pronounced a blessing upon him and said, "Your name shall no longer be Jacob but Israel for you have prevailed with God and man." Then, the angel touched his thigh and Jacob walked with a limp for the rest of his life. One of the Names of God is "El- Elyon," which means "The Most High God." So in giving him the name "Israel," God was divinely connecting Himself with Jacob's lineage for all time.

Unfortunately, not everyone is ready to deal with the deception inside themselves. I deceived myself concerning the amount of anger that was inside me. It took being bullied in a homeless shelter for the seeds to be planted in me that made take a few steps back and pray about what I was dealing with. As I did, I began listening to the feedback I was receiving. I was not just hearing who I wanted to hear or those who approached me in the way I wanted to hear it. I was listening to whomever God sent, and I was asking questions. I wanted the truth. I didn't want to be bound anymore. I was desperate to be free. This was my turning point.

I still did not see the anger in me. Different things triggered it; but I would shift the blame to other people and circumstances. I recognized the triggers but couldn't see my responsibility in them. I thought because someone or something else triggered it, that's where the fault laid. I didn't understand that I still had an obligation to respond correctly. I didn't understand what The Word of God means when it says, "Be ye angry and sin not." (Ephesians 4:26) It seemed like a contradiction to me. How do you do that? I was puzzled by Jesus turning over the moneychangers' tables in the temple (see Mark 11: 11-33; and John 2: 13- 25). I saw it as righteous anger; but what made it okay for Him to turn over their tables? If I was to do something like that, I'd never hear the end of it. I still struggle with how to respond to anger correctly; but I'm getting better. I realized I needed help when I scared my daughter during a seizure in 2017 as years of stuffed anger came up.

CHAPTER 9

"The Manipulator's Mindset"

Having a strategy is critical for many things in life. Some of those things are more important than others. Playing cards, board games, and sports may be merely entertainment for most people. Few will ever make any real money from it; and many who do, have a gambling addiction. Other people need strategies to ensure public safety in their governments and ensure the success of their business. What they do with the skills they develop determines whether they become a manipulator or whether they become a successful strategist that blesses those, they are serving.

One example of a master manipulator occurs in the book of Esther. In chapter 1, the former queen was exiled from the Persian kingdom because she didn't leave the party with her friends to meet her husband (the king) when he sent for her. To replace her, the king threw a beauty contest that Esther won; and she was chosen as his new queen, even though her people were in bondage to his. She was Jewish.

Her Uncle Mordecai, who raised her, prepared her for the contest. Shortly after that, the king whose name was Ahasuerus promoted Haman the Agagite, and set him above all the other officials. It was expected that all the king's officials would pay homage to Haman by bowing down to him; but Mordecai refused to bow because of his faith in the One true God (see Esther chapter 3). Haman was deeply offended and gave Mordecai a chance to change his mind; but Mordecai stood his ground. Once Haman found out that Mordecai was Jewish, he came up with a plot to exterminate all the Jews, to eliminate what he saw as a problem. Haman claimed the Jews had different laws and customs from the king's, making it unprofitable for the king to tolerate them. Then, Haman offered a reward from his own salary to be paid into the king's treasury for anyone who aids in the extermination of the Jews. He was the Biblical version of Adolf Hitler.

God used Esther to expose Haman's plot and save her people. At first, she was reluctant because King Ahasuerus had issued a decree that anyone who went before his presence without being summoned could be killed. The only exception was if he raised the golden scepter to them. When Haman came up with his plan and the king set his seal upon it making it a law, Queen Esther had not been summoned in three days. Nevertheless, Mordecai said to her, "Who knows if you haven't come to the kingdom for such a time as this? Do not think to yourself that in the king's palace you will escape more than all the other Jews?" (Esther 4:12) Therefore, she instructed Mordecai to have all the Jews fast on her behalf for three days as she and her young women fast in preparation for going to meet with the king. Then, Mordecai, Esther, her young women, and all the Jews fasted before she went to meet the king.

On the third day, Queen Esther went to meet King Ahasuerus. She put on her royal apparel and went to the courtyard. He was so awestruck by her beauty that he immediately extended the golden scepter. He promised her anything she wanted up to half his kingdom. Nevertheless, God had put His wisdom in her. Instead of presenting her request, she simply kept him in suspense by inviting him and Haman to a banquet she had prepared for them. Haman was ecstatic thinking that he was the guest of honor in a private feast of the king and queen. He had no idea what was coming. At the feast, they had a great time; and the king asked Queen Esther again, "What is your wish? I'll give you up to half my kingdom." She invited them to another feast. Haman went out bragging about how he was honored; and he prepared the gallows to hang Mordecai on. Meanwhile, the king had trouble sleeping. Therefore, he asked what distinction had been given to Mordecai for saving his life. Since nothing was done for Mordecai, the king asked Haman how to honor someone whom the king delights in.

Haman assumed the king was talking about him; and gave this elaborate ceremonial proclamation throughout the city square. Then, the king said, "Very well, do it for Mordecai, the Jew and leave nothing out that you have said!" Therefore, by order of the king, Mordecai's archenemy was forced to honor him. This is significant because the Lord promises to "prepare a table for us in the presence of our enemies" (see Psalm 23:5). Not long after that, it was time for Haman to meet Queen Esther and King Ahasuerus at the second feast.

During the second feast, King Ahasuerus asked Queen Esther what she wanted the third time. She knew at that point that she needed to state her concerns because he was intrigued and concerned. He knew it was something important. Therefore, in Esther chapter 7, she said, "Let my life and the life of my people be spared" (verse 3). Then, she revealed the plot against the Jews. When King Ahasuerus asked who was behind it, she confronted Haman to his face. Haman begged Queen Esther for his life while King Ahasuerus went to the palace garden to cool down; and when he returned, he saw Haman in an awkward position pleading for his life. Therefore, the gallows Haman had planned to hang Mordecai on were ordered to hang Haman on. Mordecai replaced Haman in the official office in the kingdom; and the Jews were given the right to defend themselves against the people who came to murder them.

Through this story, we see that a primary motive behind the mindset of manipulation is fear of losing political influence or power; but it is also a pride issue. It comes with a spirit of superiority. You think you are better than everyone; and you will trample all who stands in your way. You are the center of your own universe; and if people do not meet your expectations, it is their fault. If chaos occurs in your life, you believe it is always someone else's fault. You are never to blame. People must do what you want and say what you want, or they must suffer the consequences.

People who are manipulators often think this way; but they do not say these things aloud. They are not that bold. Many may not be aware they think this way. Some think they are trying to fix something that is broken. They are trying to do their part to help find a solution to a problem that is bugging them. They have no idea that they are in bondage and need to be free until God reveals it and they learn to submit it to Him. Once God reveals it, if they choose to submit it to Him, they can get free. If they choose not to submit it to Him, this problem will progress further and they will end up in deeper bondage.

When I was growing up in my parents' home, my mom and I had challenges; but my dad and I were close. Therefore, when I felt my mom was being unfair. I became a manipulator of sorts. In my plan, I went around my mom and went through my dad because I knew that I had his heart. I would tell him what I wanted, why I believed it was needed in my life, sell him on its value, and downplay its costs. If I thought it would cause a conflict between them, I left out that I had already talked to my mom. If I thought a conflict was avoidable between them, I would let him know I spoke to her. Then, I would send him in to convince my mom for me. If he was unable to convince her, he said to me, "Don't tell your mom!" and he would give it to me himself privately. It was years before I allowed God to deal with me on how much I relied on my dad to meet my needs. I was relying on my dad so much that he unknowingly got in the way of The Heavenly Father. I couldn't see it until after The Lord took him Home to Heaven. When he went Home to be with Jesus, I thought my whole world had ended. It took me a long time to move forward, which I couldn't do until I learned to make GOD Alone my Provider in all circumstances no matter what happened.

CHAPTER 10

"Mr. and Mrs. Fix-It"

Many professions require you to fix various problems. Mechanics attempt to fix people's transportation concerns. Medical professionals, attempt to fix people's physical, mental, emotional, and behavioral issues. God uses various members of the clergy (bishops, apostles, prophets, pastors, evangelists, and teachers) to help people overcome spiritual issues. Each is necessary, and can be a blessing to The Body of Christ and to those who are coming into The Body. Nevertheless, there are people, who go out of their way to fix things even when there is nothing broken. They are uncomfortable if they do not have something or someone to fix. We see many examples in Scripture.

In Genesis, God promised "Abram", whose name was changed to "Abraham" that he would be the father of many nations. He was in his nineties. Despite his age and the age of his wife "Sarai", whose name was changed to "Sarah"; he believed God, and it was credited to him as righteousness. When God told him about the lineage he would have in Genesis 15, the Lord compared it to the number of stars in the sky. Then, he had Abraham prepare an offering before Him; and the Lord proclaimed His covenant with him. In chapter 16, Sarai had convinced Abram to be intimate with her handmaiden (Hagar) because Sarai was barren. She didn't believe God's promise that she was going to produce any children for Abram, despite the covenant that God had given him. After Sarai gave Hagar to Abram, Sarai was overcome with jealousy and couldn't live with the consequences. Therefore, Sarai attempted to banish Hagar from their presence. When God changed the names of Abram and Sarai, He had called them to circumcise the child of Abram and Hagar, named Ishmael; and He renewed His covenant with Abram. By this time, Abraham was ninety-nine years old and Sarah was ninety years old. Upon hearing the news that Isaac would be born to Sarah, Abraham laughed and pronounced Ishmael as his heir.

As time went on, Sarah gave birth to their son who they named Isaac, which means "laughter". (https://www.biblegateway.com/resources/hitchcocks- bible-names-dictionary/Isaac) Once Isaac was born, Sarah became more insistent that Hagar and Ishmael leave. God wouldn't allow Hagar and Ishmael to leave until Isaac was born. He made Sarah bear the consequences of trying to fix the problem of her infertility without seeking or trusting Him for the solution.

In Exodus 32, we have a "Mr. Fix-It" who created a real mess. Moses was up on the mountain fellowshipping with The Lord God while his brother Aaron was down in the valley with the Israelites who had just been delivered from Egypt. The people got anxious and impatient because Moses was taking longer than anticipated. The people became restless and pressured Aaron to make them gods they could worship because they didn't know what happened to Moses. Aaron wanted peace at any cost and caved into the pressure. He asked the people to turn in their gold; then he made a fire and formed the gold into a calf that the people worshiped. Afterwards, they had a feast and danced around it with sacrifices. This angered the Lord God; and he got Moses' attention. He told him, "Go down to your people and stop them because they're making fools of themselves and of Me."

On Moses' way down the mountain, Joshua met him and warned him, "It sounds like war in the camp!" Moses went down to the foot of the mountain and threw the tablets of the Ten Commandments (The Lord had just given him), written with The finger of The Almighty God, onto the ground. The tablets broke at the foot of the mountain. Then, Moses took the calf they had made and burned it with fire. He ground the remains into powder and scattered it on the water. Then he made the people of Israel drink it. Then, he asked Aaron, "What did this people do to you that you have brought such a great sin upon them?" After Aaron begged for mercy from Moses, he blamed the people, failing to take responsibility for leading the people.

The problem with people inclined to fix things is many of their instincts are correct; but the way they go about it is often wrong. They are caring, compassionate people. They are family-oriented. Often they are peacemakers and peacekeepers. Many of them are extroverts, although some may be introverts. They have often been through a lot, making them empathetic. Furthermore, they generally don't ask for more respect than they are willing to give others. Despite this, they are frequently misunderstood because they sometimes don't communicate effectively. They might have difficulty knowing when they're being excessive or when they've made their point clear because they might've come from a background where they either weren't heard or felt as if they weren't. They may have been the family scapegoat so they became accustomed to taking the blame, and blame themselves for everything that goes wrong whether or not it's their fault. They feel as though if they can't fix something, it must be their fault. They may have lacked positive reinforcement growing up and might need constant positive reinforcement to encourage them so that they know they are on the right track. Therefore, they can become co-dependent on other people, instead of upon God.

A lot of this co-dependent behavior stems from fear, which is the basic root. In addition to the basic root, there is doubt. This doubt can take the form of second-guessing themselves, mistrusting others, and doubting God and His Word. This doubt can creep in because you do not trust that God is going to come through on His promises or that He will come through in a timely manner. In addition, there is a lot of insecurity because you do not see yourself as being strong enough to stand up to those you are called to lead. You prefer staying in the background. The Word of God tells us, "He has made us the head and not the tail, above only and not beneath" (see Deuteronomy 28:13).We need to take the position that He has called us into. When we are out of position, it becomes easy to sin. King David of Israel sinned with Bathsheba by having an affair with her and then having her husband murdered in battle, when King David was supposed to be in battle. If he had been in that proper position, he might not have sinned at that time (see 2 Samuel chapters 11 and 12).

God has a solution for those who want to fix things. Take it to prayer! Prayer is a powerful weapon. It changes things. Many who want to fix things are called as intercessors who stand in the gap for individuals and as spiritual watchmen who stand in the gap for groups of people. I have both callings on my life. As a spiritual watchman, I specialize in praying for governments and political officials, clergy, teachers, school officials and administrators, and businesses. I cover other areas as the Holy Spirit leads me; but those are my specialties. As an intercessor, I cover family issues, health issues, and other special concerns of people I know and don't know as they are brought to my attention. I love praising and worshipping the Lord, thanking Him for the things He has done in my life and is doing in my life. Yet, I have a difficult time asking Him for stuff for myself. It is so much easier for me to ask Him for the needs of other people than it is for me to ask for stuff for myself. I also have trouble fasting.

Therefore, when I see something I believe needs to be changed and feel it's not happening fast enough or I'm not being heard, I frequently anger people with some of the ways I try to fix things. Some of it might be in the gray area of man's conscience– not completely right, but not totally wrong. Often, I'm trying to make my point because I'm frustrated that I don't know what else to do; and if I can just have a real conversation about it with someone who will hear me and come up with alternative solutions that work for everyone, I can move forward. This is my issue and I need to deal with this correctly. I need to be free in this area; and I am submitting it to God because I know that I don't want to be back where I started when my pastor's wife inspired this book because ignoring the problem makes it worse.

CHAPTER II

"Jezebel's Deadly Heritage"

laying with yo-yos and playing tug-of-war can be fun; but they're not fun when they become part of your real-life experience. Dealing with someone who has control issues will bring you into this experience. Many with these issues are so bound that they are unaware of it themselves because of the spiritual principalities involved. Ephesians 6:12 tells us, "We do not wrestle against flesh and blood; but against principalities, against powers, against the rulers of the darkness of this world, against spiritual wickedness in high places." These are all territorial spirits; that makes them extremely controlling. If you don't have a greater authority backing you up, you will do what they want you to do and say when they want you to, or you will wish you did. One such territorial spirit is the "Jezebel" spirit.

Jezebel was **more than** an evil queen from a foreign land who worshipped pagan gods and terrorized God's chosen people, targeting the Hebrew prophets. She was so evil that when her husband was pouting over not being able to claim a vineyard he wanted because the owner refused to sell it, she had the owner killed. Then, she told her husband; go claim your vineyard, the problem has been resolved (see 1 Kings 21:1-18). A study of the book of 1 Kings reveals that Jezebel's daughter was as evil, if not worse. While I have never taken possession of anything by violent or dishonest means, I have used manipulative means in the past; and I had to repent for it.

My life has been a continuous tug-of-war, a power struggle for control. An abusive alcoholic raised my mom. My mom had terrible memories of her father's drinking; but my memories of him are more pleasant. I always thought he was drinking iced water, when in fact it was vodka over ice. To me, it didn't look any different. Because we danced to music, we played cards and we walked on the beach together; I never suspected anything. My mom inherited his illness. My mom's drink of choice was scotch over ice; but she never drank until after supper. I never saw her have more than one; but I never saw what she did after I went to bed. I never knew she was an alcoholic either.

If I said or did the wrong thing at the wrong time, even if it wasn't in front of my mom, I was in trouble. I couldn't trust anyone. I still startle easily. Because of my history with my mom, I had to learn to trust authority figures. That has been difficult. My church has helped. Prior to joining my church, the progress I've made would've been impossible because I didn't trust authority enough to let anyone help me. I've come to where I can work with those who speak to me calmly and respectfully.

I struggle with the military drill sergeant personality type. To me, they are bullies and control freaks who abuse their power and take away your choices by demanding more respect from you than they are willing to give. Generally, I have much respect for our military because they help keep our country safe; but when someone treats me like they are a military drill sergeant, I remind them I am not in the military and they are not my commanding officer. I have difficulty submitting to them. It becomes a power struggle and makes me want to rebel against them. Even when I obey them, there is usually rebellion in my heart and I am usually angry or frustrated about both my attitude and having to obey them.

Unfortunately, I am aware that giving a sacrifice of obedience with rebellion in my heart doesn't honor God. He wants us to first submit to Him, and then to those who have rule over us (see Hebrews 13:17). Nevertheless, I feel disrespected when they treat me that way. I feel like they believe I'm not important, like my thoughts and feelings don't matter; and I resent it. That is my issue to deal with.

In Matthew 5, Jesus showed us how sin begins in the heart. Proverbs 23:7 says we are what we think in our hearts. Proverbs 4:23 warns us to keep our hearts with diligence because out of it are the issues of life. Let us not forget what the prophet Samuel told King Saul of Israel, "Obedience is better than sacrifice; for rebellion is as the sin of witchcraft and presumption is as the sin of idolatry" (see 1 Samuel 15:22-23).

If we love the Lord and we want our lives to honor Him as I do, then we must allow The LORD to destroy the yoke of this bondage off our lives. There is only one way this can happen. Zechariah 4:6 tells us it is "not by might, nor by power; but by My Spirit, saith the LORD of Hosts". It requires total surrender. We must forget about what we think and how we feel. We must forget about blaming others for their treatment of us. We must keep our eyes fixed on God and Him alone. This doesn't mean we can't think about it or pray about it.

Quite the contrary, we are to cast our cares on the LORD through prayer and leave them there (see 1 Peter 5:7). Once we do that, we're not to focus on them any longer; but we are to fix our hearts and our minds on things above where Christ sits on the right hand of God (see Colossians 3:1-4; and Hebrews 12:1-2). Remember, there is a way that seems right to man; but it ends in death (see Proverbs 16:25); but the fear of the LORD is the beginning of knowledge (see Proverbs 1:7).

SECTION 3

"Totally Surrendered"

CHAPTER 12

"Creating a Kingdom-Mindset"

In the movie, "The Perfect Storm" four groups of people were trapped in the storm of the century: two teams of swordfish fishermen and women, an aircraft rescue team, and the US Coast Guard. Too many people lost their lives unnecessarily. The crew of men from the *Andrea Gail* and their sister ship from Glauster, MA were out in the storm because they put profits ahead of safety. Captain Linda Greenlaw heeded the warnings from the weatherman, directly disobeying the orders of her boat's owner who was also onboard. She saved the lives of everyone onboard her boat by asking for help. Captain Billy Tine and his crew didn't survive because they refused to listen until it was too late. The air crewmen and the Coast Guard didn't go out into the storm until they were called on the rescue mission. One hero on the rescue mission gave his life while answering the call to save others.

When you lose everything important to you, it's easy to become self-centered and shift blame; but it won't help you. The wise will rescue the foolish when they listen to wise counsel and learn from their own and others' experiences, regardless of how those experiences came about. In this section, I will share how you can shift your perspective to one that will prove most beneficial. These are the tools God gave me when I lost everything I thought was important to me. In my next book, *The Roar of the Hurricane,* I will share how this journey began and specific life lessons that empowered me to utilize the tools I needed to shift my perspective. I also share how God brought me out. No matter what you're going through, you don't have to stay stuck in a recurring cycle of frustration and despair. There's hope for you if you make the right decisions now.

Now that you have come to the place of dealing with the issues in your life instead of blaming everyone and everything else for them, you are ready to create a Kingdom-mindset. So, what does that look like practically? Having a Kingdom-mindset is about ministry. We minister first to the Lord, and then to others. Sometimes, He sends them to us; and sometimes He sends us to them. Either way, we must be open to His leading and sensitive to His direction. We must surrender to Him. In Matthew 23:36, Jesus was asked, "Master, which is the greatest commandment in The Law?" In verses 37-40, Jesus responded, "Thou shalt love the Lord thy God with all thy heart, and with all thy soul, and with all thy mind. This is the first and greatest commandment. And the second is like unto it. Thou shalt love thy neighbour as thyself. On these two commandments hang all The Law and The Prophets" (K.J.V.). Overall, this passage speaks of surrendering your will, intellect, and emotions. It is a complete surrender of your heart; but Jesus is even more practical.

The Lord wants us to understand we cannot love anyone else well until we love ourselves well. That requires learning to see ourselves the way He sees us. He formed and fashioned us in His image and likeness, according to Genesis chapters 1 and 2. We were made to be like Him. We are spirit beings in an earth suit. He uniquely gifted each of us and He has a plan and a purpose for each of our lives. When we find and fulfill the purpose He created us for, we will be filled with His blessings both in the earth and in the Heavenly realm. This is His promise.

Sometimes, people struggle because they do not see themselves as God sees them. They heard the lies of the enemy through others long enough that they started to believe them. This causes adult children to become devastated by verbal abuse. They hear the voices of the abusive parent replay repeatedly in their head each time they make a mistake and often marry someone who continues the cycle, or they continue the cycle themselves whenever they make a mistake. In some cases, both occur.

I was so used to hearing verbal abuse that I did not recognize it as abuse until I met my best friend and her family. I became verbally abusive to myself and others. If this cycle isn't broken, victims may perpetuate it in their children. Overcoming this destructive pattern requires years of meditating on Scriptures that speak of God's love and compassion for His children, renewing your mind with those Scriptures, forgiving all who hurt you including yourself, and a stubborn refusal to verbally abuse and insult yourself even when it goes against your natural instincts. You must be firmly resistant as soon as you catch yourself and say, "NO! We aren't doing that this time!" Eventually, it gets easier; and it becomes easier to see yourself the way God sees you. I had to break this pattern; and I am finally beginning to see myself the way God sees me.

As God has been healing me, one of the things I heard that I didn't initially believe but I'm beginning to recognize is, "Hurting people hurt people." Here is what I've learned. They don't know how to process their pain appropriately. All they know how to do is get rid of it, so they don't have to feel it. They think if they don't have to feel it, it will go away. What they don't understand is until they learn to process it correctly, it keeps coming back to torture them, maybe in the same form, maybe in another form; but it cycles back around (see Ecclesiastes 1:9). This is because God is a God of redemption. He loves us so much that as long as we are alive and breathing, He will always give us a chance to make things right. We are told in 2 Peter 3:9, "The Lord is not slack concerning His promise, as some men count slackness; but is longsuffering to us-ward, not willing that any should perish, but that all should come to repentance" (K.J.V.). Therefore, He is always reaching out to us. We also have an enemy who is always trying to trip us up and is trying to make us stumble.

With this kind of battle going on for our souls, is it any wonder why those who choose to ride the fence are an explosion ready to happen? The good news is that the Lord has proclaimed that He is married to the backslider in heart (see Jeremiah 3:14). As long as He keeps us alive, it's not too late to repent; but don't mess with God because He also warns us that His Spirit will not always strive with man (Genesis 6: 3). He holds death and life in His hands. If you gave your heart to Him once and are not right with Him now, get it right: long-term open rebellion, un-forgiveness, and blasphemy of the Holy Spirit can all cause you to lose your salvation (see also Revelation 3:5).

Remember, you do not get your name in "The Lamb's Book of Life" until you give your heart to Christ. If it is possible to have your name blotted out, then it has to be possible to lose your salvation. Contrast how "Pharaoh hardened his heart" in Exodus chapters 5- chapter 9, verse 7 when Moses and Aaron first appeared before him, with how "the Lord hardened Pharaoh's heart" in Exodus chapter 9, verse 8- chapter 15 when he chased the Israelites after releasing them; and notice the judgment that fell upon him.

For those of you who might say, "Well, Pharaoh was the dictator of a heathen nation that God was condemning," I offer two points. First, he still could have repented. King Nebuchadnezzar of Babylon in the time of Daniel also was the king/dictator of a heathen nation that God was condemning. God gave him space to repent; and he repented (see Daniel chapter 4). Secondly, consider Cain in the book of Genesis. He was part of the original family of Adam and Eve. They had two sons: the older was Cain and the younger was Abel. When it came time to offer up their sacrifices to God, Abel offered up the best he had, while Cain did what was convenient. When Abel's sacrifice was accepted and Cain's was rejected, Cain got jealous. That was Cain's first sin (see Genesis 4:1-7). God gave Cain space to repent; but he refused. Instead, he continued to sin and murdered his brother out of jealousy (see verses 8-12). Consequently, he was banished from the Presence of the Lord and from his family forever. Yet, even in His judgment, God is merciful. God wouldn't allow another man to retaliate. Cain had to live with the consequences for the rest of his life (see verses 13-16). There is not a positive reference to Cain in the Bible from that point forward.

Jesus spoke of un-forgiveness in Matthew 6:14-15 and of blasphemy of the Holy Spirit in Matthew 12:31-33. According to the Strong's Exhaustive Concordance of the Bible, the Greek word used for "blasphemy" in Matthew 12: 31- 33 is "blaspemia". It means "slander, malicious talk, evil speaking, or railing" (Strong, James LL.D., S.T.D.; *The Strongest Strong's Exhaustive Concordance of the Bible*; "Greek Dictionary- Index to the New Testament; Zondervan Publications; Grand Rapids, MI; 2001). God does not make it easy to lose your salvation. We have to be stubbornly rebellious to get to that level, because God is merciful and forgiving. He breathes love; but He will not violate our human will. If we make a deliberate and conscious choice to reject Him, He will leave broken-hearted and grieved. We must decide what we will do with Him. He loves us enough to respect the decision we make, even while pleading with us to make the decision that is in our best interest.

Once we have an understanding of who He created us to be and we have decided to walk in His plans and purposes for our lives, our possibilities become endless. Then, the battle really begins! We may still hear condemning and abusive voices from the past in our heads when we miss the mark; they don't quit just because we have learned to tune them out and stop repeating them. We have to process the emotions associated with them. It is painful at times. Often, we still believe those voices more than we believe what God says about us and have trouble admitting it.

We must continue to renew our minds. As we do, we learn just like Michael Jordan and Lucille Ball learned: that failure and rejection are not the end of the story. According to the "Inspirational Videos" section entitled "Dismissed" in the *Think Positive* series, Lucille Ball was "Dismissed from acting class with a note that read 'She's too shy to put her best foot forward'; and when Michael Jordan was cut from his high school basketball team, he went home, locked himself in his room and cried." Another one mentioned in that same video was President Abraham Lincoln. He failed in business twice, was defeated in eight elections, lost his fiancé, and had a nervous breakdown before he finally became President. There were others; but those three caught my attention. The video closed by saying, "If you've never failed, you've never lived. Life equals RISK!"

I never thought much of myself. I had seven chapters of my first draft written when I told one of my friends I was writing this book. She told me, "It takes people years to write books." If I had known that going in, I never would have undertaken this task because this is my first published book and I didn't think enough of myself to take on that type of challenge; but because I didn't know what to expect up-front, I was willing to do it. Now, I know, I am capable of doing this; and it is a wonderful feeling! It's amazing what you can do when you give yourself a chance. I never would have if God hadn't used my church to show me who He created me to be.

Part of renewing your mind involves stepping out because James chapter 2 tells us, "Faith without works is dead". If you believe God has put something on your heart to do, do it, even if you are afraid at first– risk it. Whatever the obstacles are, they can be overcome because God is greater than anything you see, hear, think, feel, or imagine. Ignore the skeptics. Trust God; and believe. Someone will always speak against it and try to talk you out of it. No matter what, you can't let that sway you. Stay focused on what God told you to do. God's Word will stand the test of time. God promises in Isaiah 55:5 that His Word will always accomplish what it's sent out to do; it will never return to Him empty. His Word stands the test of time because it exists outside of time. It is eternal.

Going against your skeptics is never easy. Sometimes, you face ridicule and peculiar looks. Other times, it becomes serious. Jesus told us to be ready and be on guard. In Matthew 10:24-30, Jesus said: "The disciple is not above *his* master, nor his servant above his lord. It is enough for the disciple that he be as his master, and the servant as his lord. If they have called the master of the house Beelzebub, how much more *shall they call* them of his household? Fear them not therefore: for there is nothing covered, that shall not be revealed; and hid, that shall not be known. What I tell you in darkness, *that* speak ye in the light; and what ye hear in the ear, *that* preach ye upon the housetops. And fear not them which kill the body, but are not able to kill the soul: but rather fear Him which is able to destroy both soul and body in hell. Are not two sparrows sold for a farthing? and one of them shall not fall on the ground without your Father. But the very hairs of your head are all numbered" (K.J.V.).

This persecution comes in many forms and often from those closest to us (see also Matthew 10:16- 23, and 34-36). We must count the cost (see Matthew 10:32-33, and 37-42; and Matthew 16:24-26)! If we have decided in our hearts that it's worth it to follow Him, and it is, we can't let anything or anyone stop us. We must crucify our flesh and follow Him.

Many today would like to have salvation without sacrifice; but without the sacrifice, there is no covenant. Without covenant, there is no intimacy. Without intimacy, there is no power. Jesus gave us Himself completely. Why do we want to shortchange Him? How dare we! He does not deserve that! The Apostle Paul said, "I die daily" (see 1 Corinthians 15:31). He understood that the only way to truly live was to allow Christ to live His life in him through the Holy Spirit. When I try to live my life apart from the Holy Spirit, I make a mess of things. The only way I can be happy and enjoy my life is to stay in Christ. I don't do it perfectly; but I stay in the Word, in prayer, in worship; and I stay accountable. I want to be a living sacrifice to God (see Romans 12:1-2).

The most important aspect of creating a Kingdom-mindset is having a true revelation of the authority of The Word of God, that goes beyond an intellectual assent to the truth. Anyone can agree with facts; but is it changing your life, and how you think, feel, and make decisions? That's the test! Romans 8:6 tells us, "For to be carnally minded is death: but to be spiritually minded is life and peace" (K.J.V.). What does that look like? The carnal mind has the letter of the law without the spirit of the law; and it is not mixed with faith. It becomes stale, dead religion.

The spiritual mind has it all: the letter of The Law, the Spirit of The Law, His Kingdom purpose; and it's mixed with faith. So God breathes His life into it (see Hebrews 4). We must have a firm and unwavering commitment to the Word of God and accept no other authority in our life. If someone speaks something contrary to The Word, don't do what they told you to. We must follow God! We're instructed to follow our leaders, as they follow Christ (see 1 Corinthians 11:1); but if they stray, we don't need to follow them. In my younger, more foolish years, I used that verse as an excuse for rebellion. I waited for them to do anything I disagreed with so I could claim they weren't in line with the Word, there by providing me a Biblical excuse for my rebellion because I wasn't going to rebel against God. How foolish I was! I never said anything to anyone. I just made excuses in my heart because I would never dare speak against God's chosen leaders. In my religious mindset, that was the equivalent of speaking against God. What I failed to understand then was, doing it in my heart was the same to God as doing it openly (see Matthew 5). When God says to follow our leaders as they follow Him, He doesn't intend for us to wait for them to slip so we can rebel. The spirit of The Law is to keep following Him no matter what they do; and pray that they continue to do the same. As long as they continue to, follow the leaders He gave you because they are your spiritual covering; and He put them there for your spiritual protection. Honor them with your love and prayers, and especially your submissive obedience. He established His authority in His Word so you can be a blessing to each other.

Back then, I didn't understand the purpose of spiritual authority. I thought spiritual authority was about manipulation and control. My dad was very logical and rational and my mom was very dramatic. I have elements of both to my personality. When I get frustrated, I gravitate toward my intellect. I find great comfort in thinking I can figure things out whether or not I can. It gets me in trouble spiritually because God's ways are not our ways and His thoughts are not our thoughts. His ways are higher than our ways and His thoughts than our thoughts (see Isaiah 55:8). My biggest frustration occurs when God is leading me in a certain direction but He isn't ready to give me all the information, He only gives me pieces of it. Then, I get in trouble trying to figure the rest of it out without Him. He will let me make my mistakes, wait for me to stop, and then say to me: "Are you finished (trying to figure Me out) yet?" OUCH! That is because my dad believed; "If it doesn't make sense, it can't possibly be true." Unfortunately, that does not work with God. The foolishness of God is wiser than the wisdom of men (see 1 Corinthians 1:25 and 27). Therefore, God isn't always going to make sense to my intellect; and I have to accept that. I've also had to overcome many fear and anger issues but I've overcome and I'm overcoming. You don't get to be an overcomer until you have something to overcome; and you don't get to have a testimony until you passed some tests. I'm not defeated, I'm victorious in Christ, and I'm creating a Kingdom-mindset.

Having a Kingdom-mindset is all about the authority of the Word of God. The Word of God has Its authority in the very Personhood of Christ Jesus. He is The Word of God personified. In John 1:1 we read, "In the beginning was the Word and the Word was with God, and the Word was God" (K.J.V.). Verse 14 speaks of Him putting on flesh and living with us. This is similar to the Genesis 1 account of creation in which a singular God speaks in plural terms when He says, "Let Us make man in Our image" (Genesis 1:26). Whom is He talking to? He is talking to Jesus and the Holy Spirit– the other members of the Trinity. Just as we are spirit, soul, and body– three parts making up one human being made in the image of Almighty God; They are Three holy sinless Persons making up One individual God. Some say, Jesus never claimed to be God. Jesus claimed it, using Israel's most personal covenant Name of, "I Am", attributed to God and given to Moses; and the Jews tried to stone Him for it. (See Exodus 3 and John chapter 8) Then, He proved He is God by His bodily resurrection, which was seen by many (see Matthew 28:1- 17; Mark 16:1-14; Luke chapter 24; John chapters 20-21; and Acts 1:1-9). Therefore, it is clear that The Word of God and the Person of God cannot be separated. Once you understand that, if you are a believer who accepts the authority of God in your life, you must understand the authority of The Word of God in the Kingdom of God. Just as an earthly kingdom is established upon the decrees of its king and queen, The Kingdom of God is established upon The Word of God. Those who live in the land are subject to the declarations and decrees of the land; and they can't be recognized as citizens of the land until they submit to those laws. It is the same in The Kingdom of God. The Word of God doesn't say, "Whoever recites the Sinner's Prayer shall be saved." Anybody can spout off meaningless words. It says, "If you confess with your mouth the Lord Jesus and believe in your heart that God raised Him from the dead, you shall be saved" (see Romans 10:19).

While its important what you say, its vital what you do because you prove that you believe by your actions. The Word also says, "Many are called; but few are chosen" (see Matthew 22:1-14). Jesus said we would know them by their fruits (see Matthew 7:15-27). Jesus said in Matthew 10:22 that the ones who would be saved are those who endure to the end. Those with a Kingdom mindset will endure anything to keep the Word, to minister to the Lord, and to serve all the people He has called them to.

CHAPTER 13

"Serving on God's Team"

We spoke in the last chapter about how God created each one of us for a unique and specific purpose in the earth. This is our ministry or Kingdom calling in the earth. The gifts and talents He has put in us center on the Kingdom purpose He created us for; and we should seek to align our skills to those gifts and talents. Unfortunately, many have religious mindsets when it comes to topics of faith and ministry. They tend to put God in a box and limit Him. They think of ministry as being full-time pastors, church staff, and overseas missionaries only.

No one was guiltier of disqualifying me from ministry than I was. Even professing believers in my family, gave me the impression that evangelism was to be left to the ministers in the church and to the missionaries in the foreign mission fields, because people's views of faith are "personal". If you offend them, you may keep someone who is considering faith in Christ from receiving Him. Then, you would be responsible for condemning them to Hell. I didn't want to be responsible for that. Their over-emphasis of the word "personal" was to remind me "Jesus is our Personal Lord and Savior". Our walk with God is personal; but what I didn't understand then, is when Jesus is identified as our "Personal Lord and Savior", it means that He ministers to each of us on a personal and individual level. He knows how to reach each one of us, to get us to where we need to be in Him; it doesn't mean that He is so personal that He can't be shared, like your personal identifying information. That is the impression I got within my first three months of being saved, after trying to convert my neighbors, and nearly losing all my friends, without understanding why. I was advised that if I kept quiet about my faith, I'd win my friends back; and the professing Christians in my family supported them with the misleading information about Jesus being our Personal Lord and Savior. They continued by saying, "You're not a minister; and they didn't invite you to talk about it." I asked how I would know. They responded with, "Did they ask you about your faith?" I said, "No," and they replied, "Then, they haven't invited you to talk about it." They said I could invite anybody I wanted to any church activity, especially if it is fun. After the first three months, I stopped sharing my faith with my neighborhood friends, and they all re-entered my life for a time. Once I saw that, I struggled with my walk for four and a half to five years. I, finally rededicated my life to Christ at the end of my senior year of high school and never looked back. Nevertheless, while I never had trouble inviting people to church, verbally sharing my faith was difficult.

Another roadblock to sharing my faith has been, I've had trouble seeing myself as good enough to share my faith. My perfectionist family gave me the impression that if I wasn't perfect in word and deeds (not just perfect in Christ like the Word of God speaks of), I wasn't qualified to share my faith. I felt like the rules and the boundaries were stricter for me (while having fewer privileges, rewards, and benefits for my efforts) and I deserved what I got because I had problems with my mom and couldn't figure out how to make it better. These factors silenced me. Finally, I didn't feel qualified because I was not an ordained minister who had gone to seminary.

Even though I know what I believe and can express it in print and when I'm asked specific questions; when I'm asked to start a conversation about Jesus with someone who needs the Lord, I do not know how to start the conversation. It's too much pressure. If they are willing to receive the Lord, I have no clue how to lead them in the Sinner's Prayer; I freeze up. It's frustrating! These are the anti-evangelism yokes; I struggled to overcome because Jesus gave us a Commission in Matthew 28:18-20 and Mark 16:15-18. If He didn't put conditions on that Commission, who are we to?

This doesn't undermine the role of those called into full-time Christian ministry. We need bishops, apostles, prophets, evangelists, pastors, teachers, and missionaries both in the U.S.A. and abroad. I love, respect, and appreciate them and each of their offices. However, God has a much greater need. Some need to know Him who will never step foot inside a church unless we go to them. So, the Lord places His people in every industry or occupation. For example: Luke, who wrote the Gospel of Luke, was a doctor. The Old Testament prophet, Nehemiah whom God used to rebuild the temple, was the cupbearer to a heathen king in a foreign land while Israel was in captivity. These are equally important. We are players on the same team. We must know our place and the role that God has given us. We must know our Kingdom purpose, both inside the church and in the world in which He has called us to live and work.

Discovering your Kingdom purpose is not difficult. As with anything, it starts with seeking God's face in prayer. If you open your heart and listen for His voice, He will show you. You have a primary Kingdom purpose and probably many supporting ones. What is yours? While you are seeking God, look for these clues: what do you consider yourself to be really good at; what are you passionate about; where do you get the most spiritual inspiration from when you are seeking God on things; and what do you consistently get compliments on?

For me, writing is my primary Kingdom purpose. God speaks to me more clearly, when I am writing than at any other time. That isn't to say I don't hear Him at other times; I do, but it's different when I'm writing. What makes my writing special to me is when I'm writing, I see what I'm writing before I write it. The Holy Spirit gives it to me in my head and my heart. I know it is Him because it comes in ways that I'd never think of, and often He gives me ideas I'd never think of. Furthermore, I can say things when I write that I don't have a clue how to say any other time. He amazes me!

Every time I experience this, it makes me want to write more because I want to say what He wants me say. If He hasn't given it to me in some form, I don't want to write it because it's not worth keeping. I'm His scribe, meaning I write by His assignment; I won't compromise that standard. I give that advice to you also, as you discover your Kingdom purpose. Don't compromise it for anyone or anything! Let the Holy Spirit guide you always! Only then, will you be successful! I continue learning more about my supporting Kingdom purposes.

Once you discover your Kingdom purpose, you must find your place within the Body of Christ. By now, you should be active in a local congregation. Now, you need to get involved in serving within that congregation. They need you as much as you need them. The pastoral staff, deacons, hosts, ushers, and elders cannot and should not do it alone. They haven't been called to. God "fitly joined" the Body of Christ together in love so that it would work together, to minister together and supply each other's needs– building each other up and edifying each other in love (see Ephesians 4: 16). We are to use our gifts and talents to support their ministries. In the process, we may uncover other gifts and talents we didn't know we had buried below the surface, or God may resurrect gifts and talents in us that died years ago simply because we have chosen to be faithful in using what He has given us now (see Matthew 25:14-30). No believer in Christ should be on the sidelines. We should all be active in ministry within our local congregations. Look for opportunities that match the gifts and talents God put in you; if you have concerns, talk them over with the leaders of those departments or your church leaders as the need arises.

Outside of your local congregation, God will provide ministry opportunities also. If your schedule permits, try taking on a volunteer assignment for a ministry or other charity you believe in. Let Him guide and direct your steps as to how and where to use your talents. He may even put it within your heart to take on a bigger challenge and start your own business. Whatever He is in, do it! It will succeed. If He is not in it, rethink it. We can't succeed apart from Him (see John 15:1-11); but through Him, we can do all things (see Philippians 4:13).

The attitude of our hearts as we move in what we're called to do is more important than our actions. We're called to be followers of God (see Ephesians 5:1). More than following Him, we are called to walk in His shadow (see Psalm 91). My pastor, Apostle Billy Thompson spoke on this in a message on a Sunday morning. He shared how when you start a new job, they assign someone to train you and you are to "shadow" that person. That means you are to duplicate the way they teach you to do things, according to the company's standard of doing things. We are to shadow Jesus as we see His ways of doing things laid out in The Kingdom manual or The Word of God. We are to copy His attitude, His mannerisms, His Spirit, and His actions as He gives us our assignments.

Beginning with His attitude, Jesus was all about God and people. Everything He did was filled with love. Jesus shadowed His Father; and everything He did had a Kingdom purpose. Jesus said, "I don't do anything except I see My Father in Heaven do it" (see John 5:19). Even when He turned over the moneychangers' tables, He did it to restore holiness back to God's temple and to call God's people to a place of repentance (see Matthew 21:1-46; and Mark 11:1-33). Amid His proclaiming judgment upon the religious leaders, we see Him healing the people. If we are to shadow and imitate Him, then our attitude should be to please the Father and show the love of Christ. The love of Christ is more than just "exceeding someone's expectations at customer service"; it's a love that's willing to take time to uncover what the other person needs, willing to die to its conveniences, and sacrificially meet those needs in the Name of Jesus Christ. That's the attitude we are to have.

What are the mannerisms that people think of most when they think of us? These should consistently be His mannerisms. What do they remember most about us when they leave our presence? What sticks out in their minds? If they do not see us for a long time, what do they remember about us? These are the prevailing actions that others see in us— our dominant characteristics. If we are walking in Kingdom purpose, our mannerisms should reflect this. They should be centered on Christ and His Kingdom. They should be our focus; and that focus should dictate our daily decisions and behaviors (see Colossians 3:1-3).

His Spirit must guide every decision we make. Galatians 5:16 tells us that if we walk in the Spirit, we will not fulfill the lusts of the flesh. Verses 19-21 list the actions resulting from the flesh. These are: adultery, fornication, uncleanness (or moral filthiness, particularly in the area of sexual sin), and idolatry (which is anything we make more important than God). There are others in that passage. These and other similar actions are common where the Spirit of God is not present. Many of these words are not used in American culture today; but many of the behaviors are common so people don't know how to recognize them. Galatians 5:21 tells us those who do these things will not inherit the Kingdom of God.

Galatians 5:22-23 says, "But the fruit of the Spirit is love, joy, peace, longsuffering, gentleness, goodness, faith, Meekness, temperance: against such, there is no law" (K.J.V.). These fruits must be the pattern of our lives. As His Spirit guides our lives and we have the right attitude and mannerisms, our everyday actions will eventually fall in line to match them. We're constantly growing in grace to become like Jesus as we serve Him and others.

The most important aspect of serving on God's team is positioning. If you're not positioned correctly, you won't be effective. You may be out of position in any number of areas: spiritually, emotionally, geographically, or in your assignment. Spiritually, if you don't have God's heart for the ministry assignment He has given you, like Jonah, you are out of position. Emotionally, if there are issues in your soul (will, intellect, or emotions) that need healing and you are responding to people out of that wounded soul you are out of position. You can be out of position in your assignment if you attempt to take on more than God has called you to or if you are unmotivated and are taking on less than He has called you to. You can be out of position if you are ministering in an office God has called you to; and you start thinking that it is all about you and your focus starts to shift.

When I was newly saved. I took voice lessons. I found out in 2012 that one of my voice instructors was preparing me for Broadway; but because I didn't want to practice, he gave up on me. I didn't want to practice because I didn't like the songs. Because I had grown up wanting to be the next Amy Grant (who was very popular when I was growing up) I looked for opportunities to sing solos in church all through middle school and high school. Then, when I went to college straight out of high school, I was preparing to sing a solo in my church. While I was practicing, the worship leader who was a friend that I respected, said to me: "I don't see God in this." He was the only one at the time who could've said that to me and gotten me to listen. He didn't say anything else; and I didn't question it. I went back to my dorm room and sought the Lord concerning what He meant. The Lord spoke to me, "I'm taking you off the stage. The next time you sing on stage, you'll be invited up." With the exception of my singing to my ex-husband during our wedding ceremony as a surprise, the next time I was singing on stage; I was invited up. It was not at my current church. When I asked the Holy Spirit about it, He told me clearly that the invitation would come from my current church. There are also things I know God will not release me to do until I am in the same city as my church.

Most Christians who have been saved for a long time can discern the church God called them to. How do you discern where you are to live and work, who to marry, and who to sow your financial contributions to beyond your home church? These important questions must be answered. Not hearing God can cause us to become misaligned and cause everything in our life to dry up. We need to ensure that those we are ministering to are people God's called us to; and those God's called us to partner with and fellowship with (especially our future spouse) have God's heart and are one with the purpose that God has given us. The best way to determine this as you are praying and seeking God is to do your homework. Research the companies or ministries you are interested in, learn about areas you are unfamiliar with, spend time praying for them, and see what the Holy Spirit shows you. Either He will give you a burden for that area or assignment, or He will assign someone else to it. If He gives you a burden for it, He's calling you to have a part in it. The more you pray for it, the more He will show you.

Just remember: it's His timing, not yours (see Ecclesiastes 3:11). He promises us He will guide us and show us what to do if we are seeking Him (see Psalm 32:8). Therefore, we know that the steps of the righteous are ordered by Him because they are ordered in His Word (see Psalm 37:23; and Psalm 119:133). Don't try to position yourself! You will fall on your face. Allow His Word to order your steps and His Spirit to position you. Then, everything you do will be successful and have His Kingdom blessing.

A special word that pertains to searching for a godly spouse: if you are a woman, it's not your job. The Word of God says, "Whoso findeth a wife findeth a good thing, and obtaineth favour of the LORD" (see Proverbs 18:22); and "House and riches are the inheritance of fathers: and a prudent wife is from the LORD" (see Proverbs 19:14). Both are from the King James Version. The wife is a female. Therefore, it's necessary to point out that God made man to be the pursuer and the woman to be the pursued. This doesn't mean we shouldn't be prayerful about what type of man we should allow to catch us. The man whom we should allow to catch us needs to be one who is Kingdom-minded and ministry-minded, having a servant's heart. He should be active in his home church and faithfully serving there. He should be able to provide well for any family God gives him. He should be in good standing with the leaders of his church. Furthermore, he should be one in purpose and vision with your plans and goals for the future as the Holy Spirit has revealed them to you. Anything else: is between you, your spiritual leaders, the Lord, and whomever He brings your way.

Moving onto the men, I will only say that you must be prayerful in considering your search for a godly spouse. Make sure you look for a Kingdom-minded and ministry-minded woman, having a servant's heart. She should be active in her home church and faithfully serving there. She should be in good standing with the leaders of her church. Furthermore, she should be one in purpose with your plans and goals for the future as the Holy Spirit has revealed them. Anything else: is between you, your spiritual leaders, the Lord, and whomever He brings your way. I caution you to think with your spirit as it's aligned with God's Word; and not with your will, intellect, emotions, and hormones. Put your flesh under subjection. Wait for God's timing and especially don't go pursuing a relationship before you are financially prepared to be a provider. This way if the Lord should say to you, "She's the one!" you are ready to make the commitment of a lifetime and there are no broken hearts, yours or hers.

CHAPTER 14

"Fresh Vision"

Some things about ministry are basic such as: having God's perspective, being prayed up, being bold and uncompromising with His Word in the midst of opposition, and letting His love shine in and through you regardless of your circumstances. Other things are less rigid. Remember, God is very creative. Looking at all the variations of plants and animals makes His creativity obvious. Why would we think that He would expect us whom He created in His image and likeness to be less creative? He gave a unique variety of gifts and talents to humanity and dispersed this mixture in such a way as to guarantee creativity. It was His plan for us to have fresh vision. We get our best ideas from Him. The wisest amongst us knows only ideas that come from Him have lasting value.

The most important thing to remember about ministry is that it's ministry. It's a ministry first to God and then to others He's called us to. Some have lost sight of this and made it about them. If we lose perspective, God has amazing ways of humbling us. Because I came from an upper-middle class family I had made an idol of, I thought I was too superior to associate with the "down-and-outers". Then, I faced rejection from my family. I was very class-conscious; but God humbled me and I needed it! I wouldn't wish what I went through on anyone; but it was the best thing that could've happened to me because it changed me.

It took a while for me to process all the anger in my heart correctly. Once I began taking that process seriously, my entire life changed.

One thing that helped me was the night I was venting to my pastor's wife and she let me know my perspective was way off. I was angry at everyone except God. Intellectually, I knew it didn't make sense to be mad at God, so the only reason I wasn't mad at Him was I wouldn't allow myself to become angry at the Only One Who could help me. Even though I wasn't aware of it, I had some level of control over my anger unconsciously. If I'd been conscious of that, it would've benefitted me greatly. At that point, I was angry enough that if I hadn't had the faith that He could help me; I would've been angry with Him also. I believe, she saw that and that is why she knew she could reach me that night. I don't think she would've even bothered to try if I didn't have at least that much faith. Praise God, I was in a place where she could still reach me!

Having God's perspective is critical to being able to function effectively, not just minister effectively. Life is tough! Jesus told us, "'In this world, you will have tribulation; but be of good cheer, for I have overcome the world'" (see John 16:33). Because He overcame, we can overcome. 1 Thessalonians 4:7-8 tells us God called us not to uncleanness; but to holiness and he that despises us despises God, not man, because God put His Spirit in us. This is part of what we must overcome. 1 Thessalonians 5:19 warns us to not stop the Holy Spirit from working in our lives. That is what it means to "quench" Him. When we short-circuit the Holy Spirit's work in our lives, we are the ones who lose. He has all the power to help us. We need to deal with what He calls us to deal with when He calls us to deal with it, in the manner in which He calls us to deal with it– no matter how painful the process might be.

We cannot procrastinate because procrastination makes the process more difficult in two ways. It makes us more susceptible to temptation and it makes it more difficult to deal with emotionally. This makes procrastination another thing we are called to overcome but we can do it because He lives in us. Philippians 4:13 says, "I can do all things through Christ which strengtheneth me" (K.J.V.). The last thing we are called to overcome is the tests and trials of the enemy whether they are sent to us from others we encounter, whether or not they are aware of our vulnerabilities, or whether they come from our own internal desires as James 1:12-16 warns us about.

With God's perspective, you can do amazing things. The apostles Jesus trained up in the Gospels became supernatural in the book of Acts, after the Holy Spirit descended on the day of Pentecost in Acts chapter 2. Signs and wonders followed them everywhere they went. In Acts 5:15, for example, Peter's shadow healed people because the Presence of God was so strong on him. Even Saul who was the Pharisee that held the coats of those that stoned Stephen, according to his testimony in Acts 22:20; got saved in Acts chapter 9, two chapters after Stephen was stoned. Jesus said this should be everyday life for those who follow Him (see Mark 16:15-18; Luke 10:19; and John 14:12); but Christians today, treat it as if it is strange or unusual.

This is because too many Christians are bound by their five senses. If they cannot see it, taste it, touch it, smell it, hear it, or feel it; they simply don't believe it's real. Others are bound by their intellect. If it doesn't make sense to them, if they cannot figure it out; they don't believe it is true. They forget God is above all of that. He created our five senses. He created our intellect. Certainly, He can move outside them! He doesn't need to come down to our playing field. We must come up to His (see Isaiah 55:8- 9; and Colossians 3:1-4). When we do, He will breathe His Spirit on our creative ideas and inventions. He will give us inspiration beyond our wildest dreams that will blow the minds of everyone around us; and they will be a blessing to us and all who use them. All of this will be because we chose to go beyond what our senses dictated and what made logical sense to us or anyone else; and we pressed into what we were hearing Him telling us.

So, how do we gain His perspective? There is only one place. We can go in His Presence. Psalm 91 has been favorite of mine from the time I gave my heart to the Lord; and I did not fully understand why until 2006. I always liked the poetry and the metaphors in it. It's eloquent; but it's so much more!

As the Holy Spirit was resetting my life, He opened my eyes to see what I'd never seen before. Psalm 91 is all about dwelling in the Presence of God. I finally got it one night at church when my pastor's wife and I were talking through something I had previously been concerned about. She was checking on me to see where I stood at that particular time. I said to her, "God's got this!" with full confidence. In her typical, bold prophet's fashion, she said, "Good! You have to live there! It's not enough to visit!" I immediately thought of Psalm 91; and I hadn't even read it for a while. I went back to where I was staying and read it that night. Immediately, I was struck by verse 1, which says, "He that dwelleth in the secret place of The Most High shall abide under the shadow of the Almighty." That is talking about living in the Presence of God. I started to cry. Then, I had a completely new perspective on the rest of the chapter. It was no longer just beautiful poetry that just happened to be The Word of God. It actually became Ramah to me, meaning it became personal. It was amazing!

"The Secret Place" is the most intimate place we can have with Him. In the Old Testament, the Israelites would go into the temple to worship God. The temple had several parts to it. There was the "Outer Court" where everyone gathered to fellowship and catch up on what was going on in each other's lives. Then, there was the "Inner Court" where the main congregation would gather to worship. Next was the "Holy Place", where only the priests could go and they had to bring a sacrifice. Beyond that was "The Most Holy Place" and only a few chosen priests could go in there on certain occasions. Again, a sacrifice was required. Finally, there was "The Holy of Holies". This was reserved for "The High Priest". He could only go in once a year with a sacrifice. They tied a rope to his foot because they wanted to be prepared to pull him out if he died while he was in there before the Lord; and he had to go in with a sacrifice.

Going before His Presence today requires a sacrifice of our heart. What are we willing to let go of so that we can be in His Presence? The closer we get to Him, the greater the sacrifice is required to come closer; but the rewards far outweigh the sacrifice. This is about covenant. Those who will not deny Him anything, He will not deny anything to. He already gave us Jesus, Who sacrificed His sinless Self for us because He loved us too much to live without us. Is that not worth acknowledging!

As part of the covenant we have with Him, if we choose to receive it and walk in it, we receive His covering to protect us and train us. This gives us power to do the supernatural. These are represented by His shadow. The psalmist calls the Lord a "Refuge" and "Fortress". These promise us protection from the traps of the enemy and from noisy distractions. He promises to cover us in His feathers. It reminds me of a mother hen taking her little chickens under her wings to protect them from outside dangers. His truth acts as a shield that deflects the lies of the evil one, keeping us from deception. Because of this, we don't have to fear anything that comes against us at any part of the day. We may watch casualties fall all around us who have not put their trust in the Lord; but it will not come anywhere near us. We will see the reward of the wicked from a distance because we chose to make the Lord our Refuge and The Most High our Habitation.

Also in His Presence, as part of the covenant we have with Him, we are protected from evil and illnesses. He gives His angels assignments to watch over us so we will not come into physical harm or danger. He gives us the authority to walk upon lions and snakes. We will completely trample young lions and dragons under our feet. Because we set our love upon Him, we are guaranteed His deliverance. He will elevate us because we have come into a place of intimacy with Him. When we call on Him, He will answer us. He will be with us in trouble. He will deliver us and honor us. He will satisfy us with long life and show us His salvation in ways we never expected to experience. These blessings of the covenant with the Lord are the rewards of our intimacy with Him and they are only available in His Presence.

What do we have to sacrifice? What does the Lord require? Psalm 51:17 tells us. It says, "The sacrifices of God *are* a broken spirit: a broken and a contrite heart, O God, thou wilt not despise" (K.J.V.). In Psalm 34:18, we are told, "The Lord *is* nigh unto them that are of a broken heart; and saveth such as be of a contrite spirit." According to the Strong's Exhaustive Concordance, the Hebrew word "daka" used in these two passages come from a Greek word, Each of these words speak to being crushed or destroyed. The second version even goes to the point of putting one in a crouching position. The root word form includes the word "humbled" in its definition, which is obvious from the description of these two words (Strong, James, L.L.D., S.T.D.; *The Strongest Strong's Exhaustive Concordance of the Bible*; "Hebrew-Aramaic Dictionary-Index to the Old Testament"; Zondervan Publications; Grand Rapids, MI; 2001). We must come to Him in humility and brokenness. We must be fully aware of Who He is and who we are, that we are nothing without Him. We must come to Him seeking Him for who He is, not what He can do for us. We must seek His face first, not His hand (see Matthew 6:24-34; Luke 12:1-32; and John 6:1-66).

Psalm 103:7 tells us that the Lord made His acts known to the children of Israel, and His ways known to Moses. This makes a distinction in the level of intimacy each had with their Creator. This first becomes apparent in Exodus 20:18-21. The Israelites saw the absolute majestic power of the Creator and became intimidated by it; Moses understood its purpose and encouraged them, but they refused to hear it. They allowed their fear to take them over, as I did for many years. He entered into the Presence of God, which to them appeared like a cloud of thick darkness; but to Moses who had entered in, it was a cloud of great light. God will hide Himself from those who don't want Him. No one places their most valuable treasures out in the open where they are vulnerable to any common thief that wants to steal them. They hide these treasures in dark places; and if they share them at all, they only share their most valuable treasures with those whom they have the most intimate or closest relationships with such as their friends and family. Our Creator is the same way.

This is why the religious leaders of Jesus' day who should've understood Him the most because they had the Law and the Prophets which testified of Him, understood Him the least; He is the fulfillment of them (see Matthew 5:17; and Luke 18:31). The religious leaders of Jesus' day rejected Him. We will have as much of God as we want. In James 4:8, we are told, "Draw nigh to God, and He will draw nigh to you" (K.J.V.). It is His promise. Just remember, we must do it on His terms.

The second half of James 4:8-10 gives us the criteria. It says, "Cleanse your hands, *ye* sinners: and purify your hearts, *ye* double-minded. Be afflicted, and mourn and weep: let your laughter be turned to mourning and your joy to heaviness. Humble yourselves in the sight of the Lord, and He shall lift you up" (K.J.V.). We must see our sin the way God sees it. It's not a joke to take lightly! Romans 6:23 says, "For the wages of sin *is* death, but the gift of God *is* eternal life through Jesus Christ our Lord" (K.J.V.). Every sin we commit brings us a little bit closer to death, whether we feel it or not; and it causes us to die just a little bit more spiritually. Sin carries a death sentence.

Our sin cost Jesus His life because someone had to die; it was Him or us, and He chose to be the sacrifice to save us. He knew that if we died we would be separated from Him for eternity; and He couldn't bear that. Therefore, He made the sacrifice to bring us to Him. His gift is intimacy with Him. If we don't have His perspective on our sins, we will miss the intimacy with Him that He longs to have with us.

How do we keep His perspective on our sin? We stay in His Word (see Psalm 119:11); and we stay in His Presence through prayer, praise, and worship. We must stay prayed up! Then, we allow the Holy Spirit to take us on the journey of a lifetime and enjoy the ride because it will be an adventure. As you do, He will give you fresh vision for everything you set your hand and heart to do. It won't be boring; and you will find that it's only the beginning of the tremendous impact you will have. May God bless you richly for the rest of your life.

INVITATION: A PRAYER FOR SALVATION

Dear Father God,

I know that I'm a sinner; and I've made a mess of my life. Even my righteousness, is like a dirty rag in your eyes. I know there is nothing I can do to fix it; and the harder I try, the bigger mess I seem to make. I need help, the kind of help that only You can give. I need a Savior.

I've heard about how my sins have separated me from You and about how there's no hope of redemption apart from Jesus. I also heard how You loved me too much to live without me, so You sent Jesus— Your only begotten Son— to die on the Cross in my place, even though He lived a pure and sinless life to give me an opportunity to have life with You. Thank You for loving me that much!

Now, I'm making the decision to surrender my heart and soul to You. I accept Jesus as my personal Lord and Savior this day; and I ask You to take control of my life. Make me into the person You called me to be, the person whom You had in mind when You formed me in my mother's womb. Let me see Your desire fulfilled in my life. Give me a heart to do Your will and let me follow You all the days of my life so that I may truly be prosperous in all the ways that truly matter.

Thank You for hearing my prayer, for forgiving me, for adopting me into Your family, and for giving me a new birthday as today I have been born into Your Kingdom. I'm a new creation in Christ Jesus now; and I shall follow You all the days of my life.

In Jesus' Name, I pray

Amen

REFERENCES

(1.) James, The King Version of the Holy Bible: unless otherwise noted.

(2.) "Shackles (Praise You)"; written by Atkins, Erica, Atkins, Tina, and Campbell, Warren; performed by Mary Mary; produced by Campbell, Warryn; "Thankful"; Columbia Records; (1999); retrieved from www.en.mwikipedia.org/wiki/shackles. (praise..you…)

(3.) "Waging War" written by Capehart, Christopher, Tunie, Brannon, and Winans, Ce Ce; performed by Winans, Cece; "Thy Kingdom Come"; Pure Spring Gospel Records; (2008); gmusicplus.com/cece- winans/biography/p35

(4.) "He's Able"; lyrics by: Haddon, Deitric; composed by Haddon, Dania and Haddon Deitric; produced by Haddon, Dania and Scott, Bryant; performed by The Voices of Unity Choir, featuring Darwin Hobbs; "Together in Worship"; Tyscot Records; (2007); retrieved from www.allmusic.com

(5.) James, Strong; *The Strongest Strong's Exhaustive Concordance of the Bible Hebrew-Aramaic Dictionary*; Zondervan; Grand Rapids, MI; 2001

(6.) James, Strong; *The Strongest Strong's Exhaustive Concordance of the Bible Greek Dictionary Index to the New Testament*; Zondervan Publications; Grand Rapids, MI; 2001

(7.) Think Positive. Created by Laurentiu Cocus, sponsored by Godaddy.com, Inc. retrieved from www.think-positive.us (2013/2014). Inspirational Quote from Courtney Hickman

(8.) Think Positive. Created by Laurentiu Cocus, sponsored by Godaddy.com, Inc. retrieved from www.think-positive.us (2013/2014); Inspirational Video: "Attitude Makes all the Difference" Edited by Ziglar, Zig

(9.) Think Positive. Created by Laurentiu Cocus, sponsored by Godaddy.com, Inc. retrieved from www.think-positive.us (2013/2014); Inspirational Video: "Dare to Be Great"

(10.) Think Positive. Created by Laurentiu Cocus, sponsored by Godaddy.com, Inc. retrieved from www.think-positive.us (2013/2014); Inspirational Video: "Dismissed"

(11.) Think Positive. Created by Laurentiu Cocus, sponsored by Godaddy.com, Inc. retrieved from www.think-positive.us (2013 2014); Inspirational Video: "Overcoming Adversity"

(12.) Think Positive. Created by Laurentiu Cocus, sponsored by Godaddy.com, Inc. retrieved from www.think-positive.us (2013/2014); Inspirational Video: "What They Don't Say"

(13.) Think Positive. Created by Laurentiu Cocus, sponsored by Godaddy.com, Inc. retrieved from www.think-positive.us (2013/2014); Inspirational Video; "Winning is a Habit!"

(14.) Thompson, Apostle Billy S.; 11:00 A.M., Sunday, February 23, 2014; "Identity Theft" Jesus People Proclaim International Church; Boca Raton, FL

(15.) *Hitchcock's* Bible Names; Biblegateway.Com; "Isaac"; retrieved from https://www.biblegateway.com/resources/hitchcocks-bible-names-dictionary/Isaac

(16.) "Hitchock's Bible Names, Dictionary" app updated November 17, 2017; retrieved from goroshinka2010@mail.ru

(17.) "The Names of God" app by Eric *Brou*; updated August 7, 2015; retrieved from ingenieurbrou@hotmail.com

(18.) Junger,S.(1997). *The perfect storm*. New York, NY. W.W. Norton Company